Edited by John Kendall

COMMON CORE STANDARDS

for | Middle School
English Language Arts

Susan Ryan

Dana Frazee

Alexandria, Virginia USA

Mid-continent Research for Education and Learning
Denver, Colorado USA

1703 N. Beauregard St. • Alexandria, VA 22311-1714 USA
Phone: 800-933-2723 or 703-578-9600 • Fax: 703-575-5400
Website: www.ascd.org • E-mail: member@ascd.org
Author guidelines: www.ascd.org/write

MⴊREL

Mid-continent Research for Education and Learning
4601 DTC Boulevard, Suite 500
Denver, CO 80237 USA
Phone: 303-337-0990 • Fax: 303-337-3005
Website: www.mcrel.org • E-mail: info@mcrel.org

PAPERBACK ISBN: 978-1-4166-1463-0   ASCD product #113012   n11/12

Also available as an e-book (see Books in Print for the ISBNs).

Quantity discounts: 10–49 copies, 10%; 50+ copies, 15%; for 1,000 or more copies, call 800-933-2723, ext. 5634, or 703-575-5634. For desk copies: www.ascd.org/deskcopy.

Library of Congress Cataloging-in-Publication Data
Ryan, Susan (Education standards consultant) author.
  Common core standards for middle school English language arts : a quick-start guide / Susan Ryan, Dana Frazee ; edited by John Kendall.
      pages cm
  Includes bibliographical references.
  ISBN 978-1-4166-1463-0 (pbk. : alk. paper)
1. Language arts (Middle school)—Standards. 2. Language arts (Middle school)—Curricula. 3. Lesson planning. I. Frazee, Dana, author. II. Kendall, John S., editor of compilation. III. Title.
  LB1631.R95 2012
  428.0071'2—dc23
                                                                    2012034853

22 21 20 19 18 17 16 15 14 13 12   1 2 3 4 5 6 7 8 9 10 11 12

COMMON CORE STANDARDS

STANDARDS

for | Middle School
English Language Arts

COMMON CORE STANDARDS

for | Middle School
English Language Arts

Acknowledgments

We would like to acknowledge Kirsten Miller and John Kendall for their crucial role in making our thoughts much more readable; Greg Gallagher and the North Dakota Curriculum Initiative committee, who provided us with valuable insights into the challenges facing teachers as they begin to work with the Common Core standards; Ceri Dean for her step-by-step guide to lesson planning; Kathy Olson for her collaboration and content expertise in developing the lessons; our McREL colleagues, who provided an analytical ear as we discussed the work; and our families, for supporting us as we worked on this project.

Introduction

In July 2009, nearly all state school superintendents and the nation's governors joined in an effort to identify a common set of standards in mathematics and English language arts (ELA), with the goal of providing a clear, shared set of expectations for students that would prepare them for success in both college and career. The Common Core State Standards Initiative (CCSSI) brought together researchers, academics, teachers, and others who routed multiple drafts of the standards to representatives including curriculum directors, content specialists, and technical advisors from all participating state departments of education. By spring 2010, drafts were submitted for comment to the national subject-area organizations and posted for public comment. In June 2010, the final versions were posted to a dedicated website: www.corestandards.org. (A minor update of the ELA standards was posted in October 2010.)

At press time, 46 states, as well as Washington, D.C., and two territories, have adopted the Common Core State Standards (CCSS) for English language arts. (Minnesota has adopted the ELA standards but not the mathematics standards.) Adoption of the standards is, of course, voluntary for states and does not include a commitment to any other programs or policies. However, states that have adopted these standards will be eligible to join one of two federally funded assessment consortia that are currently tasked with developing assessments for the Common Core (the Smarter Balanced Assessment Consortium [SBAC] or the Partnership for Assessment of Readiness for College and Careers [PARCC]). Sharing assessments across states promises to provide financial relief from notoriously expensive state assessments. In addition, federal programs such as Race to the Top have required that applicants demonstrate that they have joined with other states in adopting a common set of standards and an assessment program. Although states may form new consortia, many either have opted to join or are considering joining SBAC or PARCC.

Sharing a set of standards across states offers other advantages. For example, teachers' well-designed lesson plans targeting Common Core standards will be immediately useful to a large number of colleagues. The shared language of standards should also provide teachers with more opportunities to participate in very specific discussions about content, a process that has been hampered somewhat by the variety of ways states have described virtually the same content.

For a lengthier discussion of the Common Core standards, including their link to previous standards-based education efforts and the benefits and challenges the Common Core presents, see *Understanding Common Core State Standards* (Kendall, 2011). We also encourage readers to explore numerous resources available at corestandards.org, especially the standards document itself (CCSSI, 2010c), the document's appendixes (CCSSI, 2010d, 2010e, 2010f), and the guidelines for adapting standards instruction for English language learners (CCSSI, 2010a) and students with disabilities (CCSSI, 2010b).

About This Guide

This guide is part of a series intended to further the discussion and understanding of Common Core standards on a subject-specific and grade-level basis and to provide immediate guidance to teachers who must either adapt existing lessons and activities to incorporate the Common Core or develop new lessons to address new and challenging concepts not addressed in their previous state standards. After an overview of the structure of the ELA standards, we examine the middle school standards in depth, describing how they are designed to help students build upon and extend skills acquired in earlier grades. Next, we focus on practical lesson planning with the Common Core, looking at a process for creating lessons that make the best use of the effective instructional strategies explored in *Classroom Instruction That Works, 2nd edition* (Dean, Hubbell, Pitler, & Stone, 2012). The guide concludes with an illustration of this process's outcome: three sample lessons that address standards identified as representing notable changes to teachers' current practice.

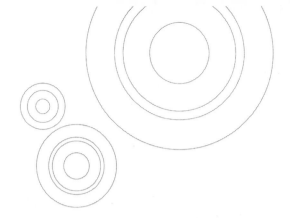

CHAPTER 1

About the Common Core English Language Arts Standards for Middle School

This chapter focuses on key areas of the Common Core State Standards for English language arts that represent the most significant changes to commonly used curricula and presents an overview of how the standards are organized, fit together, and reinforce one another. Reviewing the essential student knowledge and skills in the Common Core will allow teachers to quickly understand how they might adjust the materials and strategies used in their classroom to best meet these new expectations.

Focus Areas and Instructional Implications

Although the Common Core ELA standards are comprehensive and address a broad range of communication skills, they place particular emphasis on five key areas: reading informational text, reading complex text, close reading and citing text evidence, writing arguments, and research. Let's take a closer look at each area and consider its implications for teachers.

Reading informational text

During the last decade, the amount of nonfiction included in literature textbooks and on national reading tests such as the National Assessment of Educational Progress (NAEP) has been increasing. The Common Core adds momentum to this trend, calling for a balance between literature and informational texts in the curriculum. The standards also emphasize domain-specific vocabulary and informative writing, requiring that students read texts that provide rich subject-area content and models of expository structures. Considering that as little as 15 percent of current middle school instructional reading is expository (Common Core State Standards Initiative, 2010d), adoption of the Common Core standards means middle school teachers will need to increase the number of informational texts read in their classrooms.

Reading complex text

The Common Core defines a three-part model for selecting texts in each grade span that will lead to college and career readiness by the end of high school. Within this model, text readability—specifically, its quantitative measure for relative difficulty—is set higher than the mark set by prior readability systems and reading comprehension assessments for each grade span. Middle school students are now expected to independently read and understand texts with Lexile scores between 925 and 1185L by the time they finish 8th grade (Nelson, Perfetti, Liben, & Liben, 2012), which is notably higher than prior expectations (860–1010L) (CCSSI, 2010d). This change will have a strong impact on which texts, and in particular which informational texts, are appropriate for middle school students. The qualitative measures and reader task considerations—the other two legs in the model for text selection in the Common Core—provide teachers with a set of criteria to use when evaluating titles for particular students and situations. For a complete description of the Common Core's text complexity model, please see Chapter 2.

Close reading and citing text evidence

The Common Core has numerous reading standards that ask students to closely analyze the information, ideas, and rhetorical choices that appear in texts. Students are expected to provide text evidence to support their assertions about the content and rhetoric in texts that they read. Teachers may emphasize this type of close reading and use of text evidence in their classrooms by increasing the number of text-based questions that they ask. Currently, many questions in the curriculum are designed to develop student background knowledge or to help students make connections between the text and their prior experience. These types of questions will remain important during pre-reading exercises and as support strategies, but the bulk of questions used should be text-based. Text-based questions can be answered only by careful examination of the text. The Common Core publishers' criteria document (Coleman & Pimentel, 2012) estimates that 80 to 90 percent of questions within the curriculum should be text-based to match the requirements of the Common Core reading standards. Additionally, teachers should favor graphic organizers and activities that ask students to provide direct quotations from the text as evidence. Teachers may want to immediately begin to inventory and review their current curriculum to identify and modify the types of questions and organizers used.

Writing arguments

Many of the Common Core ELA standards ask students to evaluate and develop formal, logical arguments based on text evidence. While prior state standards typically described a broad set of skills related to persuasion, they did not place particular emphasis on dissecting logical arguments. Teachers will need to incorporate lessons that ask students to analyze exemplar oral and written arguments, and they will need to increase the number of writing and speaking assignments in which students argue their opinion about a topic or theme, using text-based evidence as support.

Research

The research standards in the Common Core are not a significant departure from those found in most state standards, and most teachers may find that they are accustomed to covering similar content during the course of a year. However, the Common Core specifies that students conduct both brief and sustained research and that this research be woven into many different classroom contexts. Likewise, standards throughout the Common Core reflect research skills requiring students to compare and integrate information from diverse sources. Teachers seeking to implement the Common Core standards will likely need to increase the number of activities in which students gather and synthesize information.

How the Standards Are Organized

The Common Core ELA standards present content within a highly organized structure, first by strands and then by more specific headings. The standards themselves provide the most detailed level of content description: statements of student knowledge and skills for particular grades. In middle school, there are standards for grades 6, 7, and 8. Each grade-level content standard can be traced back to the Common Core's foundation: the set of College and Career Readiness Anchor standards (CCRA) that broadly describe what students should know and be able to do by the time they graduate high school. To further clarify the structure of the Common Core standards, we will look at each organizational category in turn.

Strands

The ELA standards are sorted into four strands: Reading, Writing, Speaking and Listening, and Language. The first three of these categories will be familiar, as they have been used to organize content in numerous state ELA standards documents. The category of Language, however, is found less frequently in state standards. The Common Core Language strand describes skills that may be applied to one or more of the other strands. For example, grammar may be applied to both writing and speaking activities, and vocabulary is an important element of reading, writing, speaking, and listening. The strands are also distinguished from some state standards in that research skills and media literacy are not separate categories; research is addressed in the Common Core Writing strand, and media is embedded throughout the ELA strands, with some emphasis in the Speaking and Listening strand. At the middle school and high school levels, the Reading strand is further subdivided into two domains: the Reading Standards for Literature and the Reading Standards for Informational Text. The standards in these two domains are parallel, addressing the same basic reading skills but describing them in ways specific to reading fiction versus reading literary nonfiction.

Each strand has an associated abbreviation code to identify its particular numbered standards, with each of the two domains of the Reading strand receiving its own shorthand:

- Reading Literature (RL)
- Reading Informational Text (RI)
- Writing (W)
- Speaking and Listening (SL)
- Language (L)

These strand abbreviations are used as part of the CCSSI's official identification system, which provides a unique identifier for each standard in the Common Core and can be very useful to school staffs developing crosswalks, planning lessons, and sharing lesson plans. For example, the third standard in the Writing strand can be referred to as "Writing Standard 3" or, using the full, formal "dot notation," as "CCSS.ELA-Literacy.W.3." To speak specifically of a standard for a particular grade level, the grade designation is inserted between the strand letter and standard number: "CCSS.ELA-Literacy.W.6.3," for example, is Writing Standard 3 for grade 6. In this guide, we use an abbreviated form of this identification system, dropping the common prefix and using strand and standard number (e.g., W.3.). In the sample lessons, we insert the grade level indicator.

Headings

Within each strand, a set of two or more topic headings provide further organization. The same headings span all grade levels. In the Language strand, for example, the standards are organized under three headings: Conventions of Standard English, Knowledge of Language, and Vocabulary Acquisition and Use. The headings provide users with an overview of the topics that the particular strands address, group standards that share a similar focus, and provide context for understanding individual standards. For example, the Craft and Structure heading in the Reading strand signals that the standards listed under it will focus on the various choices that authors make when developing (crafting) and organizing (structuring) their writing.

College and Career Readiness Anchor standards

As noted, the College and Career Readiness Anchor standards define the knowledge and skills students should acquire in each content strand over the course of their K–12 education. The more specific, grade-level content standard statements spell out the aspects of CCRA knowledge and skills appropriate for students within that grade band. In other words, there is a version of every anchor standard for each grade level, and every grade level has the same anchor standards. For illustration, see Figure 1.1, which displays the 6th, 7th, and 8th grade versions of the same anchor standard within the Reading strand.

In this way, the anchor standards provide overarching goals for student learning. When a single standard includes many details and various aspects, teachers can identify that standard's primary focus by reviewing

Figure 1.1 | **Middle School Grade-Specific Versions of a CCRA Standard**

CCRA:	Grade 6 Students:	Grade 7 Students:	Grade 8 Students:
RL.2 Determine central ideas or themes of a text and analyze their development; summarize the key supporting details and ideas.	**RL.6.2** Determine a theme or central idea of a text and how it is conveyed through particular details; provide a summary of the text distinct from personal opinions or judgments.	**RL.7.2** Determine a theme or central idea of a text and analyze its development over the course of the text; provide an objective summary of the text.	**RL.8.2** Determine a theme or central idea of a text and analyze its development over the course of the text, including its relationship to the characters, setting, and plot; provide an objective summary of the text.

its associated anchor standard. The progression of grade-level standards provides a structure that indicates how students' skills are expected to advance over time. As teachers assess their students, the continuum of grade-level standards in the Common Core may enhance their understanding of how student skills develop. Additional assistance can be found in a learning progression framework developed by the National Center for the Improvement of Educational Assessment, which identifies research-based learning progressions for use with the Common Core (Hess, 2011).

Connections Across Content Areas

It is important to note that the Common Core ELA standards are published in the same document as the Common Core Literacy Standards for History/Social Studies, Science, and Technical Subjects. Because the literacy standards are intended for teachers in those subject areas, rather than language arts teachers, we do not address them within this guide. However, the Common Core emphasizes an integrated model of literacy that includes cross-subject collaboration among teachers, so language arts teachers will benefit from familiarizing themselves with the literacy standards. Briefly, the literacy standards cover reading and writing and share the same CCRA standards as the ELA standards; the grade-specific literacy standards describe how the same set of skills articulated in the ELA standards should be applied in social studies, science, and technical classrooms.

Appendices to the ELA/Literacy Standards

In addition to the standards themselves, the Common Core standards document for ELA includes a set of three appendices that provide further clarification and support.

Appendix A (CCSSI, 2010d) explains the research base and rationale for many of the key aspects of the standards. It describes how to use the Common Core text complexity model, which includes three factors for determining the appropriate complexity of texts for each grade range. Appendix A also describes the three major text types required by the standards in the Writing strand: argument, exposition, and narration. The role of oral language in literacy is also described, as are various aspects of the Language strand, including vocabulary.

Appendix B (CCSSI, 2010e) provides further support related to text complexity by excerpting portions of particular texts that illustrate the level of complexity required of students within each grade band. Middle school has one text complexity band for grades 6–8. Short performance tasks accompany the exemplar texts and indicate the types of activities and student performances that support specific reading standards.

Appendix C (CCSSI, 2010f) provides annotated samples of student writing for each grade level that meet or exceed the minimum level of proficiency the standards demand. Examples are provided across all three of the text types: argument, informational/expository, and narrative writing. In most cases, the samples are accompanied by a description of the context for writing (prompt, requirements, audience, and purpose). Annotations help clarify how the sample meets the requirements of the grade-level standards.

* * *

As noted, our intention in this guide is to provide readers with a sense of the meaning of each middle school ELA standard and explain how the standards are related to each other across both grade levels and strands. Readers should be aware that what we present are examples of such connections; we do not mean to suggest that no other connections can or should be made. Teachers should build on the information here to strengthen their own practice and enhance their implementation of the Common Core standards.

Now that we've looked at the overall structure of the Common Core ELA standards, we will examine each strand in turn.

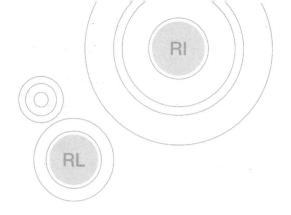

CHAPTER 2

Reading

The Common Core standards expect students to read both widely and deeply. Students read across a variety of genres and time periods to develop cultural appreciation and insights into the human condition. At the same time, they read materials deeply, thinking critically about the presented concepts and dissecting the author's execution of his or her craft. As discussed later in this chapter, a key aspect of the standards is that they provide an opportunity for all students to encounter and learn from complex texts that prepare them for the level of reading required in college and careers.

Both of the consortia currently designing assessments for the Common Core standards, the Smarter Balanced Assessment Consortium and the Partnership for Assessment of Readiness for College and Careers, have announced that they plan to assess mastery of the reading standards using selected-response items, such as multiple choice, and constructed-response items that require short or long written responses. SBAC will use computer adaptive testing for its interim and summative reading assessments for the purpose of providing educators and parents with specific information about each student's reading level. Similarly, PARCC is developing a reading diagnostic assessment as an optional tool to help educators identify students' independent reading levels.

The Reading strand is divided into two domains: the Reading Standards for Literature ("reading literature" or "RL") and the Reading Standards for Informational Text ("reading informational text" or "RI"). Each of these domains shares the same College and Career Readiness Anchor standards and the same four headings: Key Ideas and Details, Craft and Structure, Integration of Knowledge and Ideas, and Range of Reading and Level of Text Complexity. The reading literature standards and reading informational text standards share a number of similarities. In this chapter, we'll review both domains, alternating our focus between them as we move from one heading to the next, using excerpts from the Common Core as the basis for discussion.

Key Ideas and Details

The Common Core authors note that the standards ask students to "read like a detective" (Coleman & Pimentel, 2012, p. 16). Detective readers carefully review the content, structure, and rhetorical techniques in a text for clues to its meaning. This type of investigation is at the heart of the reading standards, beginning with the Key Ideas and Details heading. Figure 2.1 shows the sequence of standards in the reading literature domain. Differences in each standard's phrasing from the prior grade level are shown in boldface text to highlight how the standard's content changes from grade to grade.

Phrased identically in the literature and informational text domains, Reading Standard 1 (abbreviated as RL.1 and RI.1, respectively) provides a foundation for the Common Core focus on students' close, analytic reading and gathering of supporting text evidence. The majority of standards in the Reading strand ask students to analyze or evaluate texts, and this first standard requires them to thoroughly support those analyses with text evidence. In this way, it works in tandem with many of the other standards that follow. Across grades, Reading Standard 1 also requires students to comprehend texts and make inferences when reading.

Reading Standard 1 describes a continuum of advancing skill related to students' ability to support their ideas about books. By 7th grade, students are expected to find several quotations or details from their reading to support their ideas. By 8th grade, they are asked to select from a body of evidence the particular details that provide the best support for their opinions. Across the middle school grades, Reading Standard 1 also requires students to grasp explicit ideas and details in texts and make logical inferences about what they read. The ability to comprehend and make inferences is closely tied to the particular text's level of difficulty (see the discussion of Reading Standard 10, beginning on p. 26, for more details on determining the appropriate grade-level texts for middle school students).

RL.1–3

Figure 2.1 ǀ **Reading Literature Standards 1–3: Key Ideas and Details**		
Grade 6 Students:	Grade 7 Students:	Grade 8 Students:
RL.1 Cite textual evidence to support analysis of what the text says explicitly as well as inferences drawn from the text.	**RL.1** Cite **several pieces of** textual evidence to support analysis of what the text says explicitly as well as inferences drawn from the text.	**RL.1** Cite **the** textual evidence **that most strongly supports an** analysis of what the text says explicitly as well as inferences drawn from the text.
RL.2 Determine a theme **or central idea of a text and how it is conveyed through particular details;** provide a summary of the text **distinct from personal opinions or judgments.**	**RL.2** Determine a theme or central idea of a text and **analyze its development over the course of the text;** provide an objective summary of the text.	**RL.2** Determine a theme or central idea of a text and analyze its development over the course of the text, **including its relationship to the characters, setting, and plot;** provide an objective summary of the text.
RL.3 Describe how a particular story's or drama's plot unfolds in a series of episodes as well as how the characters respond or change as the plot moves toward a resolution.	**RL.3 Analyze how particular elements of a story or drama interact (e.g., how setting shapes the characters or plot).**	**RL.3** Analyze how **particular lines of dialogue or incidents in a story or drama propel the action, reveal aspects of a character, or provoke a decision.**

Note: Boldface text identifies content that differs from the prior grade level.

The next two standards under this heading describe the ways in which students are expected to closely analyze written content, including its key ideas and details.

Reading Standard 2 (RL.2/RI.2) asks students to draw conclusions about the central idea or themes in a text and summarize them, using text details rather than their own opinions as support. The only difference between the literature and informational text versions of this standard is the inclusion of "themes" in literature. As they do with all skills addressed in the ELA standards, students build facility with text analysis over the course of their K–12 education. They begin in their elementary years by summarizing main ideas and details. By 6th grade, they are able to distinguish between ideas explicit in the text and their own interpretations, and they can clearly summarize a text using details provided in the text without injecting their personal opinions. In 7th grade, students support conclusions about how a theme is developed in a text. Throughout middle school, they select text details to include in summaries and find details that support their conclusions about the book's central theme.

Reading Standard 3 (RL.3/RI.3) focuses on the interaction and development of key ideas and details within a text. This standard differs significantly from grade to grade and between its iterations in the reading literature and the reading informational text domains, so we'll discuss it using the more specific nomenclature.

At grade 6, Reading Literature Standard 3 focuses on plot development—how events build in a story. At grade 7, the same standard focuses on the interaction of setting, characters, and plots, and at grade 8, it focuses on the effects of dialogue and plot events. At every middle school grade level, students studying these elements are expected to highlight, quote, and cite details from the text to support their ideas. Teachers accustomed to using graphic organizers and note-taking techniques that require students to quote descriptions, events, and dialogue from the text will find that these tools remain useful for addressing Reading Literature Standard 3.

Figure 2.2 shows the full sequence of standards under Key Ideas and Details within the reading informational text domain.

Figure 2.2 | **Reading Informational Text Standards 1–3: Key Ideas and Details**

Grade 6 Students:	Grade 7 Students:	Grade 8 Students:
RI.1 Cite textual evidence to support analysis of what the text says explicitly as well as inferences drawn from the text.	**RI.1** Cite **several pieces** of textual evidence to support analysis of what the text says explicitly as well as inferences drawn from the text.	**RI.1** Cite the **textual evidence that most strongly supports** an analysis of what the text says explicitly as well as inferences drawn from the text.
RI.2 Determine **a central idea of a text** and how it is conveyed through particular details; provide a summary of the text **distinct from personal opinions or judgments.**	**RI.2** Determine **two or more** central ideas in a text and **analyze their development over the course of the text;** provide an **objective** summary of the text.	**RI.2** Determine a central idea of a text and analyze its development over the course of the text, **including its relationship to supporting ideas;** provide an objective summary of the text.
RI.3 Analyze in detail how a key individual, event, or idea is introduced, illustrated, and elaborated in a text (e.g., through examples or anecdotes).	**RI.3** Analyze the **interactions between** individuals, events, and ideas in a text **(e.g., how ideas influence individuals or events, or how individuals influence ideas or events).**	**RI.3** Analyze **how a text makes connections among and distinctions between** individuals, ideas, or events **(e.g., through comparisons, analogies, or categories).**

Note: Boldface text identifies content that differs from the prior grade level.

As previously noted, the first two standards are identical, or nearly identical, to the versions in the reading literature domain, addressing textual evidence and analyzing main ideas and details, respectively. Reading Informational Text Standard 3 (RI.3), however, differs from its counterpart in reading literature. This standard focuses on how ideas and details in a text are related, and the requirements of this standard at each grade vary. In 6th grade, students focus on how

For a lesson addressing Reading Informational Text Standards 2 and 3 at the 7th grade level (RI.7.2–3), see **Sample Lesson 2.**

details in a book or article convey the work's central ideas and concepts. In 7th grade, students consider how ideas and details are connected, such as in cause-and-effect relationships. And in 8th grade, students study how authors categorize and compare ideas and details.

The standards under the Key Ideas and Details heading all relate to comprehending and citing the main ideas and supporting details in texts, as well as analyzing how those ideas and details relate to one another and accomplish the author's purposes. As with all of the Common Core standards in the Reading strand, increased difficulty from one grade to the next is directly related to the increasing complexity of the text being analyzed, an aspect that is described in detail within the discussion of standards under the Range of Reading and Level of Text Complexity heading (see p. 26).

Notably, the reading standards do not specify the use of particular reading comprehension strategies (such as making predictions), as is common in many state standards documents. The Common Core publishers' criteria document for ELA and literacy states that "to be effective, instruction on specific reading techniques should occur when they illuminate specific aspects of a text. Students need to build an infrastructure of skills, habits, knowledge, dispositions, and experience that enables them to approach new challenging texts with confidence and stamina. As much as possible, this training should be embedded in the activity of reading the text rather than being taught as a separate body of material" (Coleman & Pimentel, 2012, p. 9). Thus, reading strategies are left to classroom teachers to model and incorporate into instruction as driven by curricula and student needs.

Craft and Structure

The three standards under the Craft and Structure heading require students to evaluate the techniques and strategies that authors employ in texts, analyzing diction, organization, and point of view or purpose. Figure 2.3 shows the sequence of these standards for reading literature.

Figure 2.3 | **Reading Literature Standards 4–6: Craft and Structure**

Grade 6 Students:	Grade 7 Students:	Grade 8 Students:
RL.4 Determine the meaning of words and phrases as they are used in a text, including figurative **and connotative meanings; analyze the impact of a specific word choice on meaning and tone.**	**RL.4** Determine the meaning of words and phrases as they are used in a text, including figurative and connotative meanings; **analyze the impact of rhymes and other repetitions of sounds (e.g., alliteration) on a specific verse or stanza of a poem or section of a story or drama.**	**RL.4** Determine the meaning of words and phrases as they are used in a text, including figurative and connotative meanings; analyze the impact **of specific word choices on meaning and tone, including analogies or allusions to other texts.**
RL.5 Analyze how a particular sentence, chapter, scene, or stanza fits into the overall structure of a text and contributes to the development of the theme, setting, or plot.	**RL.5** Analyze **how a drama's or poem's form or structure (e.g., soliloquy, sonnet) contributes to its meaning.**	**RL.5 Compare and contrast the structure of two or more texts and analyze how the differing structure of each text contributes to its meaning and style.**
RL.6 Explain how an author develops the point of view of the narrator or speaker in a text.	**RL.6 Analyze** how an author develops **and contrasts** the points of view **of different characters or narrators** in a text.	**RL.6** Analyze how **differences in the points of view of the characters and the audience or reader (e.g., created through the use of dramatic irony) create such effects as suspense or humor.**

Note: Boldface text identifies content that differs from the prior grade level.

The first standard here, Reading Literature Standard 4 (RL.4), focuses on diction—the explicit and implied meaning of words authors use. The focus in 6th grade is how word choices affect meaning and tone, the focus in 7th grade is word choices in poetry, and the focus in 8th grade is analogies and allusions. (Analogies and allusions are also the target of RI.4 at the grade 8 level; see below.)

The second standard under this heading, Reading Literature Standard 5 (RL.5), examines how stories and poetry are structured. In grade 6, students learn how sentences, chapters, scenes, or stanzas fit together; in grade 7, students focus on dramatic and poetic forms; and in grade 8, students compare and analyze the structure of two or more literary texts.

Reading Literature Standard 6 (RL.6) is about point of view. Prior to middle school, students learn to identify and compare point of view across literary texts. Beginning in grade 6, students analyze point of view as an author's creation, noting how it is developed (grade 6), how a character's point of view compares to other characters' points of view in the same text (grade 7), and how a character's point of view compares to the readers' perspectives (grade 8). As with all the reading standards, RL.6 requires students to support their assertions about point of view with specific evidence, quoting and referencing details in the text.

Figure 2.4 shows the standards under the Craft and Structure heading for the reading informational text domain. While they closely resemble their counterparts for reading literature, they include details specific to reading literary nonfiction.

For a lesson addressing Reading Informational Text Standards 2 and 3 at the 8th grade level (RI.8.2–3), see **Sample Lesson 3**.

Reading Informational Text Standard 4 (RI.4) is phrased fairly similarly to RL.4, asking students to study figurative uses of words, connotations, and technical meanings in context. In grade 7, students must also analyze the overall impact of word choices, and in grade 8, students study specific words and phrases that make allusions or analogies.

Reading Informational Text Standard 5 (RI.5) focuses on the structure and organization of informational texts. In middle school, students study how words, sentences, paragraphs, chapters, and sections are organized to guide the reader. Many teachers are accustomed to using activities to help students identify how nonfiction texts are organized (e.g., creating an outline of information as they read,

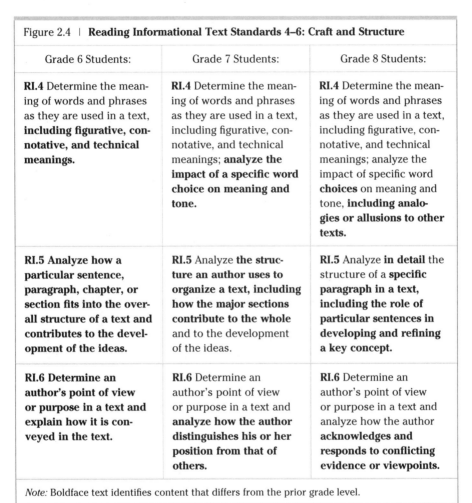

Figure 2.4 | **Reading Informational Text Standards 4–6: Craft and Structure**

Grade 6 Students:	Grade 7 Students:	Grade 8 Students:
RI.4 Determine the meaning of words and phrases as they are used in a text, **including figurative, connotative, and technical meanings.**	**RI.4** Determine the meaning of words and phrases as they are used in a text, including figurative, connotative, and technical meanings; **analyze the impact of a specific word choice on meaning and tone.**	**RI.4** Determine the meaning of words and phrases as they are used in a text, including figurative, connotative, and technical meanings; analyze the impact of specific word **choices** on meaning and tone, **including analogies or allusions to other texts.**
RI.5 Analyze how a particular sentence, paragraph, chapter, or section fits into the overall structure of a text and contributes to the development of the ideas.	**RI.5** Analyze **the structure an author uses to organize a text, including how the major sections contribute to the whole** and to the development of the ideas.	**RI.5** Analyze **in detail** the structure of a **specific paragraph in a text, including the role of particular sentences in developing and refining a key concept.**
RI.6 Determine an author's point of view or purpose in a text and explain how it is conveyed in the text.	**RI.6** Determine an author's point of view or purpose in a text and **analyze how the author distinguishes his or her position from that of others.**	**RI.6** Determine an author's point of view or purpose in a text and analyze how the author **acknowledges and responds to conflicting evidence or viewpoints.**

Note: Boldface text identifies content that differs from the prior grade level.

highlighting topic sentences); however, the Common Core standards in middle school ask students to go a step further and analyze how the organization is embedded throughout the work as a whole and how that organization supports the author's intended meaning. Thus, middle school teachers might ask students to review, summarize, and draw conclusions about the structures used in informational texts.

As noted, RL.6 focuses on the effects of a chosen point of view. Similarly, its counterpart, Reading Informational Text Standard 6 (RI.6), asks 6th grade students to determine the author's point of view and purpose by examining textual details. In grade 7, they move on to analyzing how the author makes his or her purpose or point of view clear and distinct—different from the purpose of point of view of another. Teachers may choose to highlight the author's choices by asking students to compare nonfiction works that have similar themes but different purposes or reflect different perspectives. At grade 8, RI.6 focuses on how authors respond to opposing ideas. This content can be addressed efficiently through the study of informational texts that present an argument, such as editorials or speeches.

Integration of Knowledge and Ideas

The Integration of Knowledge and Ideas heading covers standards that focus on students' comparing and synthesizing the ideas and information from different works, including multimedia and artistic mediums. Figure 2.5 shows the sequence of these standards for reading literature.

For a lesson addressing Reading Literature Standard 7 at the 6th grade level (RL.6.7), see **Sample Lesson 1.**

The standards under this heading focus on comparing multiple texts. (Note that Standard 8, which is about evaluating arguments, is found only in the reading informational text domain.) The first standard, Reading Literature Standard 7 (RL.7), asks students to compare content presented in different media and formats. Students in 6th grade compare the experience of reading a specific text with the experience of listening to or viewing a "performed" version. Students in 7th grade compare written texts to live or recorded versions, studying audio and visual communication techniques. Students in 8th grade take this comparison of audio and visual communication a step further by considering an evaluative component.

In Reading Literature Standard 9 (RL.9), students analyze themes and topics across multiple texts, focusing on differences among forms and genres (grade 6); differences among fiction and historical accounts (grade

RL.7 & RL.9

Figure 2.5 | **Reading Literature Standards 7 and 9: Integration of Knowledge and Ideas**		
Grade 6 Students:	Grade 7 Students:	Grade 8 Students:
RL.7 Compare and contrast **the experience of reading a story, drama, or poem to listening to or viewing an audio, video, or live version of the text, including contrasting what they "see" and "hear" when reading the text to what they perceive when they listen or watch.**	**RL.7** Compare and contrast **a written story, drama, or poem to its audio, filmed, staged, or multimedia version, analyzing the effects of techniques unique to each medium (e.g., lighting, sound, color, or camera focus and angles in a film).**	**RL.7 Analyze the extent to which a filmed or live production of a story or drama stays faithful to or departs from the text or script, evaluating the choices made by the director or actors.**
RL.8 (Not applicable to literature)	**RL.8** (Not applicable to literature)	**RL.8** (Not applicable to literature)
RL.9 Compare and contrast texts **in different forms or genres (e.g., stories and poems; historical novels and fantasy stories)** in terms of their approaches to similar themes and topics.	**RL.9** Compare and contrast **a fictional portrayal of a time, place, or character and a historical account of the same period as a means of understanding how authors of fiction use or alter history.**	**RL.9 Analyze how a modern work of fiction draws on themes, patterns of events, or character types from myths, traditional stories, or religious works such as the Bible, including describing how the material is rendered new.**

Note: Boldface text identifies content that differs from the prior grade level.

7); and connections among contemporary and traditional works, such as archetypes (grade 8). The 8th grade emphasis on allusion is supported by other 8th grade standards in the Reading strand that specify the study of analogies and allusions (RI.3 and RI.4; RL.4) and is further developed in the reading standards for grades 9–10, when students are asked to analyze literary allusions and assess how texts build and transform ideas found in prior works. At all grade levels, curricular units that address Reading Standard 9 should provide students with opportunities to read and compare a variety of works—short and long texts, fiction and nonfiction—that address the same themes, topics, or time periods.

Figure 2.6 shows standards under the Integration of Knowledge and Ideas heading in the reading informational text domain. Similar to their counterparts in the reading literature domain, these three standards focus on synthesizing and evaluating information from texts. RI.8 adds evaluating logic and arguments in literary nonfiction.

Reading Informational Text Standard 7 (RI.7) focuses on comparing works that contain information on the same subject or topic but present that information in different manners. The grade 6 standard includes a clear link to the research process and to the standards under the Research to Build and Present Knowledge heading within the Writing strand (see W.7–9, p. 42) in that students build knowledge by synthesizing information from multiple print and media sources. The grade 7 standard asks students to compare print and media versions of the same text, and the grade 8 standard adds an evaluative component to the comparison by asking students to assess how well various formats present a topic or idea.

Reading Information Text Standard 8 (RI.8), which appears only in the reading informational text domain, focuses on evaluating the logic and reasoning an author uses. It is a key standard, reflecting the Common Core's emphasis on students' ability to dissect and develop arguments. In middle school, this standard includes identifying supporting evidence in a text (grade 6) and evaluating the quality of the evidence supporting a claim (grades 7–8). Later, in high school, RI.8 asks students to take their assessment of argumentation further by identifying false statements and fallacious logic in historic and U.S. legal documents.

Reading Informational Text Standard 9 (RI.9), the final standard under the Integration of Knowledge and Ideas heading, is similar to its reading literature counterpart in that students analyze texts with shared themes or topics. In grade 6, RI.9 focuses on comparing various texts that describe the same event. In grade 7, it asks students to compare authors' evidence

Figure 2.6 | Reading Informational Text Standards 7–9: Integration of Knowledge and Ideas

Grade 6 Students:	Grade 7 Students:	Grade 8 Students:
RI.7 Integrate information presented in different media or formats (e.g., visually, quantitatively) as well as in words to develop a coherent understanding of a topic or issue.	**RI.7 Compare and contrast a text to an audio, video, or multimedia version of the text, analyzing each medium's portrayal of the subject (e.g., how the delivery of a speech affects the impact of the words).**	RI.7 Evaluate the advantages and disadvantages of using different mediums (e.g., print or digital text, video, multimedia) to present a particular topic or idea.
RI.8 Trace and evaluate the argument and specific claims in a text, distinguishing claims that are supported by reasons and evidence from claims that are not.	RI.8. Trace and evaluate the argument and specific claims in a text, **assessing whether the reasoning is sound and the evidence is relevant and sufficient to support the claims.**	RI.8 **Delineate** and evaluate the argument and specific claims in a text, assessing whether the reasoning is sound and the evidence is relevant and sufficient; **recognize when irrelevant evidence is introduced.**
RI.9 Compare and contrast one author's presentation of events with that of another (e.g., a memoir written by and a biography on the same person).	**RI.9 Analyze how two or more authors writing about the same topic shape their presentations of key information by emphasizing different evidence or advancing different interpretations of facts.**	RI.9 Analyze a case in which **two or more texts provide conflicting information on the same topic and identify where the texts disagree on matters of fact or interpretation.**

Note: Boldface text identifies content that differs from the prior grade level.

and interpretation of facts related to a topic. In grade 8, RI.9 focuses on analyzing conflicting information found in two or more texts on the same topic. Across the grade levels, this standard requires teachers to carefully select reading materials to ensure the texts will elicit the types of comparisons called for. Remember that an important premise of the Common Core standards is that as teachers across the country work to develop curricula based on the standards, they will create a collection of shareable, high-quality materials that both evoke the thoughtful comparisons described in Reading Informational Text Standards 7, 8, and 9 and demonstrate sufficient complexity for the grade band, as described below.

Range of Reading and Level of Text Complexity

The final heading within the Reading strand covers just a single standard. Reading Standard 10 (RL.10/RI.10) reflects the idea that students must apply their developing reading skills to texts that increase in complexity each year to ensure that they will graduate prepared to read entry-level college texts.

It's important to say a few words here about the Common Core text complexity model, which includes three factors: qualitative measures, quantitative measures, and reader and task considerations. These factors are described in detail within Appendix A (CCSSI, 2010d), with models provided in Appendix B (CCSSI, 2010e).

Quantitative measures are objective and may be evaluated using a readability measure, which calculates text difficulty by examining aspects such as word and sentence length. Six different measures for calculating readability were compared in a recent study (Nelson et al., 2012), and these measures now share a common scale that aligns to college and career readiness as described in the Common Core. These measures include ATOS®, Degrees of Reading Power®, Flesch Kincaid®, Lexile framework®, Source Rater©, and Pearson Reading Maturity Metric©. Quantitative readability measures do not address drama and poetry, however, and are less accurate for literature than they are for informational texts.

The other factors in the text complexity model are more subjective. Qualitative factors include aspects of the text such as levels of meaning, structure, language conventionality and clarity, and knowledge demands. Rubrics have been developed by the Kansas State Department of Education (2011) and the National Center for the Improvement of Educational Assessment (Hess & Hervey, 2011) to assess qualitative factors for literature and informational text. These same groups have developed criteria to aid teachers considering the third component of Common Core text complexity, reader and task considerations. This final aspect of the model takes into account students' individual motivation, knowledge, and experiences, as well as the complexity of the assignment. As more educators work to implement the Common Core standards in the coming years, additional tools to aid teachers in evaluating text complexity and selecting appropriate texts for classroom use will likely be developed.

Within the Reading strand, both the standards for reading literature and the standards for reading informational text describe text complexity in terms of grade bands. In middle school, there is a single grades 6–8 text complexity band. It's expected that students in 6th and 7th grade may need supports, such as guided reading, to read texts at the high end of the 6–8 text complexity band—and that all students will be able to read these texts independently by the end of 8th grade.

The publisher's criteria for the ELA Common Core standards indicate that when students need supports to access a complex text above their reading level, teachers should ask questions that guide students to find the answer in the text rather than answer the students' questions by explaining the text to them. Pre-reading supports that build students' background knowledge should concentrate on words and concepts that are important to understanding the text and that cannot be derived through the context of the text itself. The degree of support provided to students should correspond to their individual needs, and particular attention should be paid to designing supports for English language learners and other students who struggle with complex texts (Coleman & Pimentel, 2012).

Figure 2.7 shows the Range of Reading and Level of Text Complexity standard for reading literature (RL.10). In addition to describing text complexity, RL.10 describes the range of student reading by identifying a variety of genres that students should be exposed to, including stories, dramas, and poetry. Stories appropriate to grades 6–12 are further defined as adventure stories, historical fiction, mysteries, myths, science fiction, realistic fiction, allegories, parodies, satire, and graphic novels. Drama

RL.10

Figure 2.7 | **Reading Literature Standard 10: Range of Reading and Level of Text Complexity**

Grade 6 Students:	Grade 7 Students:	Grade 8 Students:
RL.10 By the end of the year, read and comprehend literature, including stories, dramas, and poems, in the grades 6–8 text complexity band proficiently, with scaffolding as needed at the high end of the range.	**RL.10** By the end of the year, read and comprehend literature, including stories, dramas, and poems, in the grades 6–8 text complexity band proficiently, with scaffolding as needed at the high end of the range.	**RL.10** By the end of the year, read and comprehend literature, including stories, dramas, and poems, **at the high end of** the grades 6–8 text complexity band **independently and proficiently.**

Note: Boldface text identifies content that differs from the prior grade level.

includes one-act and multi-act plays in written and oral forms. Poetry includes poems written in narrative, lyrical, and free-verse forms; sonnets; odes; ballads; and epics.

Figure 2.8 shows the Range of Reading and Level of Text Complexity standard for reading informational text (RI.10). It mirrors RL.10, using identical phrasing to describe text complexity. In regard to the appropriate range of reading, RI.10 defines informational texts for grades 6–12 as literary nonfiction, which includes exposition, argument, and functional text in the form of personal essays; speeches; opinion pieces; essays about art or literature; biographies; memoirs; journalism; and historic, scientific, technical, or economic accounts (including digital sources) written for a broad audience. Although literary nonfiction includes genres that are structured similarly to narratives, such as biographies, the standards emphasize nonfiction that is built on informational text structures, such as essays and speeches. Informational documents that are not designed for a wide audience, such as technical reports, should be taught in other subject-area classrooms using the literacy standards for social studies, science, and technical subjects.

Across grade levels and domains, Reading Standard 10 has clear implications for curriculum and instruction. It calls for teachers to select a

Figure 2.8 ǀ **Reading Informational Text Standard 10: Range of Reading and Level of Text Complexity**		
Grade 6 Students:	Grade 7 Students:	Grade 8 Students:
RI.10 By the end of the year, read and compre-hend literary nonfiction in the grades 6–8 text complexity band profi-ciently, with scaffolding as needed at the high end of the range.	**RI.10** By the end of the year, read and compre-hend literary nonfiction in the grades 6–8 text complexity band profi-ciently, with scaffolding as needed at the high end of the range.	**RI.10** By the end of the year, read and compre-hend literary nonfiction **at the high end** of the grades 6–8 text complex-ity band **independently and proficiently.**

Note: Boldface text identifies content that differs from the prior grade level.

variety of reading materials that encompass both the breadth and the com-plexity described in the standards. The *PARCC Model Content Frameworks* (PARCC, 2011) suggests that unit plans include a variety of short texts that complement longer texts. For example, short informational texts might build the background knowledge needed to analyze a historical novel. Short texts also may provide greater opportunity for students to reread, which in turn supports the type of close, analytic examination essential to many of the reading standards. Short complex texts, or short excerpts from longer texts, may be used to model reading strategies and analytic thinking. The mix of short and longer texts will also provide opportunities for students to engage with texts of varying levels of complexity.

While Reading Standard 10 is clear that all students should build pro-ficiency with grade-level complex texts and topics, students also need opportunities to build fluency and vocabulary with texts that they can comprehend independently. Essentially, the Common Core calls for teach-ers to use the text complexity model to carefully select reading materials of various lengths, genres, and complexity, which will provide all students with the opportunity to increase their reading ability and prepare for the challenges of college or the workplace.

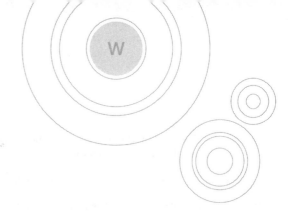

CHAPTER 3

Writing

The Common Core writing standards describe three types of writing: argument, exposition, and narration. They also encompass skills related to writing processes, including using technology and conducting research. Taken together, the standards emphasize writing as a tool that develops students' critical thinking and learning.

Standards in the Writing strand (W) are grouped under four headings: Text Types and Purposes, Production and Distribution of Writing, Research to Build and Present Knowledge, and Range of Writing. Our discussion is organized by heading.

Both consortia that are developing assessments for the Common Core will assess student writing. As currently described, SBAC will ask students to demonstrate their ability to write a variety of short pieces (one or more paragraphs) and longer pieces (planned and developed over multiple sessions) for different purposes and audiences. In addition, students will respond to at least one extended performance task that may draw on a variety of reading, writing, speaking, and research skills. PARCC will assess students' writing as part of its performance-based assessment, which will focus on writing effectively when analyzing text. Both consortia are likely to employ a mix of computer and human scoring to evaluate student writing.

Technical aspects of student writing, such as correct use of English conventions, will be assessed not only through student performance tasks and constructed-response items but also through computer-based selected-response items, such as multiple choice. Skills related to using correct grammar and conventions are part of the Language strand of the Common Core standards because they pertain to both writing and speaking; see Chapter 5 for a full description of grammar and conventions for writing.

Text Types and Purposes

Across all grades, there are three primary types of writing described under the Text Types and Purposes heading: argumentation, exposition, and narration. For the first two writing types, students write organized, content-based paragraphs to support a claim or main idea. The reading standards' emphasis on reading informational texts that model both nonfiction structures and a formal tone will help students better understand how to write about information and ideas. For the third writing type, narration, students write a story, organized by a plot and featuring effective use of story elements. The Common Core standards call for the same balance of writing types found in the NAEP. In middle school, the allocation is 35 percent argument, 35 percent informative, and 30 percent narrative (National Assessment Governing Board, U.S. Department of Education, 2011).

Although the standards describe just three types of writing, they also indicate that as students address specific purposes and audiences, they will employ a wide variety of forms or subgenres, such as speeches, investigative reports, literary analysis, summaries, and research papers.

Notably, the standards do not dictate the length or particular format for writing within each text type, such as a five-paragraph essay for informative writing. They focus, rather, on the characteristics that each text type of student writing should exhibit in order to develop the topic or story in a clear and coherent way. Not only should students be flexible in their ability to use different formats and subgenres, but Appendix A of the standards document notes that effective student writing may blend text types to accomplish a given purpose, such as when an essay or speech includes a personal anecdote to illustrate a point. Effective writing assignments will provide students with opportunities to write in a variety of forms and will be flexible in how they allow students to apply characteristics from various writing types to best meet a given purpose and audience.

The standards under the Text Types and Purposes heading, Writing Standards 1–3, are very specific, and each has numerous components that describe the attributes of that type of writing. Some of the attributes described in each standard's components are shared across more than one writing type and standard, while others are specific to that standard alone. For example, when students are writing arguments and when they are writing about information, they are expected to "Establish and maintain a formal style" (Standards W.1d and W.2e). These components provide the descriptions of and details about proficient student writing that might be useful in developing writing rubrics. The attributes that appear across standards—text introduction, ideas and content, organization, word choice, tone, and conclusion—reflect the elements used in generic rubrics developed by SBAC: content focus, organization, and elaboration, as well as use of conventions, language, and vocabulary (Measured Progress & ETS Collaborative, 2012). With the exception of conventions, which are described in the Language strand, these elements correspond roughly to the components organized under each Text Types and Purposes standard.

The writing standards under the Text Types and Purposes heading change across grades, describing proficiency at each grade for each writing type. The standards in 6th grade, for example, reflect significantly different phrasing than the 5th grade standards that precede them. Although the skills described at the 5th and 6th grade levels are clearly related, students entering middle school are expected to generate more complex writing structures and engage in more nuanced analysis of writing choices than their elementary school peers. Differences in the standards' phrasing in the 6th, 7th, and 8th grades are more subtle, as we will now see.

Writing arguments

The first writing standard focuses on writing arguments by supporting an opinion with clear reasons and evidence. Appendix A cites a variety of research that identifies argumentation as a key skill for college readiness. It also draws a distinction between argument and persuasion. While argument is solely about making appeals to logic, persuasion also includes appeals to emotion and ethics. Lack of reference to persuasion in the standards adds emphasis to the relative importance of evidence-based arguments, but students will need to call upon a range of rhetorical skills to serve a variety of purposes and audiences. Indeed, students must recognize emotional and ethical appeals in the arguments and texts that they analyze and construct, as well as understand the difference between facts and opinions. Figure 3.1 shows Writing Standard 1 (W.1) across grades 6, 7, and 8.

As students enter middle school, they begin to develop more formal arguments. In the elementary grades, they learned to support their opinions with reasons and information, but in middle school, they are asked to make specific thesis statements and more clearly define their claims in relation to alternate or opposing ideas.

At the middle school level, Standard W.1 stresses that the evidence students use to support their claims must be drawn from credible sources and should be deliberately selected to demonstrate their understanding of the topic. This standard clearly supports research skills in that it asks student to evaluate sources and synthesize information drawn from these sources (see the discussion of Writing Standards 7, 8, and 9, beginning on p. 41, for more details about the research skills required of students).

As students progress through middle school, the organization of their writing must be not only clear but also thoughtfully and logically structured to define and defend a particular claim. In elementary school, students learned to use transitional words, phrases, and clauses to link opinions and reasons; now, in middle school, they are asked to use these devices to clarify more complex relationships among claims, counterclaims, and

Figure 3.1	**Writing Standard 1: Text Types and Purposes—Argumentation**		
Grade 6 Students:	Grade 7 Students:	Grade 8 Students:

W.1 Write **arguments to support claims with clear reasons and relevant evidence.**
    a. Introduce **claim(s) and organize the reasons and evidence clearly.**
    b. **Support claim(s) with clear reasons and relevant evidence, using credible sources and demonstrating an understanding of the topic or text.**
    c. Use **words, phrases, and clauses to clarify the relationships among claim(s) and reasons.**
    d. **Establish and maintain a formal style.**
    e. Provide a concluding statement or section **that follows from the argument presented.**
	W.1 Write arguments to support claims with clear reasons and relevant evidence.
	    a. Introduce claim(s), **acknowledge alternate or opposing claims,** and organize the reasons and evidence **logically.**
	    b. Support claim(s) with **logical** reasoning and relevant evidence, using **accurate,** credible sources and demonstrating an understanding of the topic or text.
	    c. Use words, phrases, and clauses to **create cohesion** and clarify the relationships among claim(s), reasons, **and evidence.**
	    d. Establish and maintain a formal style.
	    e. Provide a concluding statement or section that follows from and **supports** the argument presented.
		W.1 Write arguments to support claims with clear reasons and relevant evidence.
		    a. Introduce claim(s), acknowledge and **distinguish** the claim(s) from alternate or opposing claims, and organize the reasons and evidence logically.
		    b. Support claim(s) with logical reasoning and relevant evidence, using accurate, credible sources and demonstrating an understanding of the topic or text.
		    c. Use words, phrases, and clauses to create cohesion and clarify the relationships among claim(s), **counterclaims,** reasons, and evidence.
		    d. Establish and maintain a formal style.
		    e. Provide a concluding statement or section that follows from and supports the argument presented.

Note: Boldface text identifies content that differs from the prior grade level.

evidence. Beginning in 6th grade, students are asked to write using a formal style and to close their writing by drawing all of the evidence together into a logical conclusion that supports their claims.

Writing informative or explanatory texts

The second standard under Text Types and Purposes, Writing Standard 2 (W.2), focuses on exposition. Writing about information helps students build knowledge across a wide spectrum of topics and subjects, and this standard complements the Common Core reading standards that ask students not only to comprehend key ideas and details but also to integrate, connect, and analyze information from multiple sources. By writing explanatory texts, students exhibit their ability to think critically about information.

Appendix A of the standards document describes a variety of genres that should be included in expository writing, such as academic reports, analyses, summaries, workplace documents, and functional writing. Just like Writing Standard 1, Writing Standard 2 asks students to draw detailed information from sources to support the ideas in their writing. Students must select, organize, and analyze content on the subject in order to write clearly about it. Figure 3.2 shows the sequence of the Writing Standard 2 across the middle school grades. Like Writing Standard 1, Writing Standard 2 features components that describe the characteristics of proficient writing, including introductions and organization, supporting details, transitions, word choice, tone, and conclusions.

In elementary school, students learned to logically group content to organize their informative writing. Now, in middle school, they learn that the ways in which they organize their writing should be adjusted to match the growing complexity of the subjects they study (and will need to write about). In grades 6 and 7, students are asked to structure their writing by defining key aspects of the subject, classifying information about the subject, comparing pieces of information, or describing cause-and-effect relationships. With these foundational skills, students in grade 8 are better able

W.2

Figure 3.2 ǀ **Writing Standard 2: Text Types and Purposes—Informative Writing**		
Grade 6 Students:	Grade 7 Students:	Grade 8 Students:
W.2 Write informative/explanatory texts to examine a topic and convey ideas, **concepts,** and information **through the selection, organization, and analysis of relevant content.** a. Introduce a topic; **organize ideas, concepts, and information, using strategies such as definition, classification, comparison/ contrast, and cause/ effect;** include formatting (e.g., headings), **graphics (e.g., charts, tables),** and multimedia when useful to aiding comprehension. b. Develop the topic with relevant facts, definitions, concrete details, quotations, or other information and examples. c. **Use appropriate transitions to clarify the relationships among ideas and concepts.** d. Use precise language and domain-specific vocabulary to inform about or explain the topic. e. **Establish and maintain a formal style.** f. Provide a concluding statement or section **that follows from** the information or explanation presented.	**W.2** Write informative/explanatory texts to examine a topic and convey ideas, concepts, and information through the selection, organization, and analysis of relevant content. a. Introduce a topic **clearly, previewing what is to follow;** organize ideas, concepts, and information, using strategies such as definition, classification, comparison/contrast, and cause/ effect; include formatting (e.g., headings), graphics (e.g., charts, tables), and multimedia when useful to aiding comprehension. b. Develop the topic with relevant facts, definitions, concrete details, quotations, or other information and examples. c. Use appropriate transitions to **create cohesion and** clarify the relationships among ideas and concepts. d. Use precise language and domain-specific vocabulary to inform about or explain the topic. e. Establish and maintain a formal style. f. Provide a concluding statement or section that follows from and **supports** the information or explanation presented.	**W.2** Write informative/explanatory texts to examine a topic and convey ideas, concepts, and information through the selection, organization, and analysis of relevant content. a. Introduce a topic clearly, previewing what is to follow; organize ideas, concepts, and information **into broader categories;** include formatting (e.g., headings), graphics (e.g., charts, tables), and multimedia when useful to aiding comprehension. b. Develop the topic with relevant, **well-chosen** facts, definitions, concrete details, quotations, or other information and examples. c. Use appropriate **and varied** transitions to create cohesion and clarify the relationships among ideas and concepts. d. Use precise language and domain-specific vocabulary to inform about or explain the topic. e. Establish and maintain a formal style. f. Provide a concluding statement or section that follows from and supports the information or explanation presented.

Note: Boldface text identifies content that differs from the prior grade level.

to generalize about information from the details and structure their writing into broad categories. When appropriate, students may choose to display content and information in tables, charts, and multimedia, which implies familiarity with word processing and presentation software.

Similar to W.1, W.2 requires students writing about information to use transitional words and phrases to help the reader understand the relationships among ideas and information. In 7th grade, the focus for transitions is on creating cohesion, while in 8th grade, the focus is on varying the transitions used. When writing about information, students are asked to choose precise words and phrases that convey a very specific meaning, including domain-specific vocabulary, or technical words related to a specific subject. Such word choices will help student writers establish a formal tone and style. Middle school students are expected to bring closure to their writing by drawing conclusions that follow and support the writer's main ideas about the topic.

Writing narratives

The third standard under the Text Types and Purposes heading describes narration, or storytelling. Students write about experiences, either real or imaginary. In contrast to the first two writing types, narration is structured by time and place. Narrative writing may serve a variety of purposes and appear in a variety of formats, including narrative poems, essays, and short stories. Such writing increases students' appreciation of the literary techniques they encounter when reading, which suggests that students may benefit from studying the content under the Craft and Structure heading of the reading literature domain (RL.4–RL.6, see p. 19) as they learn how and where to employ these techniques. Narrative writing also provides students with the opportunity to engage in their learning by expressing their personal ideas, culture, and experiences. Figure 3.3 shows the sequence of Writing Standard 3 (W.3) across grades 6, 7, and 8.

Overall, the middle school versions of this standard ask students to think about their audience and apply their insight to craft an engaging story. They are expected to structure and pace their stories so that readers

W.3

Figure 3.3 ǀ **Writing Standard 3: Text Types and Purposes—Narration**		
Grade 6 Students:	Grade 7 Students:	Grade 8 Students:

W.3 Write narratives to develop real or imagined experiences or events using effective technique, **relevant** descriptive details, and **well-structured** event sequences.
  a. **Engage and** orient the reader by establishing a **context** and introducing a narrator and/or characters; organize an event sequence that unfolds naturally **and logically.**
  b. Use narrative techniques, such as dialogue, pacing, and description, to develop experiences, events, and/or characters.
  c. Use a variety of transition words, phrases, and clauses to **convey** sequence and **signal shifts from one time frame or setting to another.**
  d. Use precise words and phrases, **relevant descriptive details,** and sensory language to convey experiences and events.
  e. Provide a conclusion that follows from the narrated experiences or events.
	W.3 Write narratives to develop real or imagined experiences or events using effective technique, relevant descriptive details, and well-structured event sequences.
	  a. Engage and orient the reader by establishing a context and **point of view** and introducing a narrator and/or characters; organize an event sequence that unfolds naturally and logically.
	  b. Use narrative techniques, such as dialogue, pacing, and description, to develop experiences, events, and/or characters.
	  c. Use a variety of transition words, phrases, and clauses to convey sequence and signal shifts from one time frame or setting to another.
	  d. Use precise words and phrases, relevant descriptive details, and sensory language to **capture the action** and convey experiences and events.
	  e. Provide a conclusion that follows from and **reflects** on the narrated experiences or events.
		W.3 Write narratives to develop real or imagined experiences or events using effective technique, relevant descriptive details, and well-structured event sequences.
		  a. Engage and orient the reader by establishing a context and point of view and introducing a narrator and/or characters; organize an event sequence that unfolds naturally and logically.
		  b. Use narrative techniques, such as dialogue, pacing, description, and **reflection,** to develop experiences, events, and/or characters.
		  c. Use a variety of transition words, phrases, and clauses to convey sequence, signal shifts from one time frame or setting to another, **and show the relationships among experiences and events.**
		  d. Use precise words and phrases, relevant descriptive details, and sensory language to capture the action and convey experiences and events.
		  e. Provide a conclusion that follows from and reflects on the narrated experiences or events.

Note: Boldface text identifies content that differs from the prior grade level.		

can follow the events and characters easily and to use narrative techniques, such as dialogue, to support that engagement. In 6th and 7th grades, students use transition devices that signal a change in time or place. By 8th grade, they are asked to include more reflection in their stories and employ transitions that convey the relationships among experiences and events. Students are asked to craft descriptions that are precise and relevant; by 7th grade, it's expected they will be able to engage their audience by selecting words that capture the action and draw their readers in.

Production and Distribution of Writing

While the first group of standards in the Writing strand details the qualities and characteristics of different writing types, the remaining standards focus on writing processes. The three standards under the Production and Distribution of Writing heading, shown in Figure 3.4, address adapting writing to task, purpose, and audience; using the writing process; and using technology.

The first standard here, Writing Standard 4 (W.4), requires students to adapt their writing for specific tasks, purposes, and audiences. It acknowledges that students need to be flexible writers who can adjust their selected details, text structure, and style to meet the demands of a given writing task. W.4 is uniform across grades 6–12; the difficulty level of the skill increases with the demands and complexity of the contexts that students address in their writing.

Writing Standard 5 (W.5) focuses on the writing process. While Writing Standard 10 (see p. 44) makes it clear that students need not apply the full writing process to everything they write, students do need practice planning, revising, and editing their written work. In elementary school, it's a given that students will receive guidance and support from peers and adults during the writing process. This level of support is scaled back when students reach middle school, and focus shifts to developing their ability to produce polished writing on their own, when support is not available. Standard 5 states that students in grades 6–8 receive "some support," which is generally interpreted to include scaffolding such as prewriting

Figure 3.4 ǀ **Writing Standards 4–6: Production and Distribution of Writing**		
Grade 6 Students:	Grade 7 Students:	Grade 8 Students:
W.4 Produce clear and coherent writing in which the development, organization, **and style** are appropriate to task, purpose, and audience.	**W.4** Produce clear and coherent writing in which the development, organization, and style are appropriate to task, purpose, and audience.	**W.4** Produce clear and coherent writing in which the development, organization, and style are appropriate to task, purpose, and audience.
W.5 With **some** guidance and support from peers and adults, develop and strengthen writing as needed by planning, revising, editing, rewriting, or trying a new approach.	**W.5** With some guidance and support from peers and adults, develop and strengthen writing as needed by planning, revising, editing, rewriting, or trying a new approach, **focusing on how well purpose and audience have been addressed.**	**W.5** With some guidance and support from peers and adults, develop and strengthen writing as needed by planning, revising, editing, rewriting, or trying a new approach, focusing on how well purpose and audience have been addressed.
W.6 Use technology, including the Internet, to produce and publish writing as well as to interact and collaborate with others; demonstrate sufficient command of keyboarding skills to type a minimum of **three** pages in a single sitting.	**W.6** Use technology, including the Internet, to produce and publish writing and **link to and cite sources** as well as to interact and collaborate with others, **including linking to and citing sources.**	**W.6** Use technology, including the Internet, to produce and publish writing and **present the relationships between information and ideas efficiently** as well as to interact and collaborate with others.

Note: Boldface text identifies content that differs from the prior grade level.

exercises and editing checklists. By the time they reach high school, students are expected to produce multiple drafts without directed guidance and support. Here in middle school, they prepare to meet that challenge by learning how to rewrite and refine their writing, working independently. While all writers benefit from an editor, reviewers are not always available to writers in all situations; for this reason, students need opportunities to practice revising their work without the frame of a writing workshop or peer review. As is noted in the Common Core standards document, editing skills should match the convention and grammar rules specified in the Language standards.

Finally, Writing Standard 6 (W.6) asks students to use technology to produce and publish individual and collaborative writing. In prior grade levels, this standard specifies that students be able to do this with guidance and support; beginning in grade 6, students are expected to be able to use technology independently and with increased efficiency. For example, W.6 at the 5th grade level requires students to generate a minimum of two pages of typed text in a single sitting; at the 6th grade level, that minimum increases to three pages. In grade 7, it is expected that students will be able to use technology to link to and cite sources. In grade 8, they are asked to begin to experiment with technology to present information and ideas in ways best suited to the content, which may mean inserting bookmarks or links within a document or using tables and graphs.

Research to Build and Present Knowledge

In the Common Core standards, research is more than a type of assignment; it is described as a set of skills that may be applied, as needed, to many different types of reading, speaking, listening, and writing tasks. Although the standards under the Research to Build and Present Knowledge heading articulate specific aspects of research processes, the basic skill of synthesizing text information from multiple sources is embedded in many different standards across the ELA strands. In response to this emphasis on research skills, both consortia developing assessments for the Common Core have designed items to test students' research skills, including performance-based tasks that ask students to select appropriate sources and synthesize information.

The three standards listed under Research to Build and Present Knowledge, shown in Figure 3.5, address the scope and purpose of research projects, gathering and synthesizing source information, and the use of analytical reading skills to draw text evidence.

W.7–9

Figure 3.5 | **Writing Standards 7–9: Research to Build and Present Knowledge**

Grade 6 Students:	Grade 7 Students:	Grade 8 Students:
W.7 Conduct short research projects **to answer a question, drawing on several sources and refocusing the inquiry when appropriate.**	**W.7** Conduct short research projects to answer a question, drawing on several sources and **generating additional related, focused questions for further research and investigation.**	**W.7** Conduct short research projects to answer a question **(including a self-generated question),** drawing on several sources and generating additional related, focused questions **that allow for multiple avenues of exploration.**
W.8 Gather relevant information from **multiple** print and digital sources; **assess the credibility of each source; and quote** or paraphrase **the data and conclusions of others while avoiding plagiarism and providing basic bibliographic information for sources.**	**W.8** Gather relevant information from multiple print and digital sources, **using search terms effectively;** assess the credibility and accuracy of each source; and quote or paraphrase the data and conclusions of others while avoiding plagiarism and **following a standard format for citation.**	**W.8** Gather relevant information from multiple print and digital sources, using search terms effectively; assess the credibility and accuracy of each source; and quote or paraphrase the data and conclusions of others while avoiding plagiarism and following a standard format for citation.
W.9 Draw evidence from literary or informational texts to support analysis, reflection, and research. a. Apply *grade 6 reading standards* to literature (e.g., **"Compare and contrast texts in different forms or genres [e.g., stories and poems; historical novels and fantasy stories] in terms of their approaches to similar themes and topics.").** b. Apply *grade 6 reading standards* to literary nonfiction (e.g., **"Trace and evaluate the argument and specific claims in a text, distinguishing claims that are supported by reasons and evidence from claims that are not.").**	**W.9** Draw evidence from literary or informational texts to support analysis, reflection, and research. a. Apply *grade 7 reading standards* to literature (e.g., **"Compare and contrast a fictional portrayal of a time, place, or character and a historical account of the same period as a means of understanding how authors of fiction use or alter history.").** b. Apply *grade 7 reading standards* to literary nonfiction (e.g., **"Trace and evaluate the argument and specific claims in a text, assessing whether the reasoning is sound and the evidence is sufficient to support the claims.").**	**W.9** Draw evidence from literary or informational texts to support analysis, reflection, and research. a. Apply *grade 8 reading standards* to literature (e.g., **"Analyze how a modern work of fiction draws on themes, patterns of events, or character types from myths, traditional stories, or religious works such as the Bible, including describing how the material is rendered new.").** b. Apply *grade 8 reading standards* to literary nonfiction (e.g., **"Delineate and evaluate the argument and specific claims in a text, assessing whether the reasoning is sound and the evidence is relevant and sufficient; recognize when irrelevant evidence is introduced.").**

Note: Boldface text identifies content that differs from the prior grade level.

Writing Standard 7 (W.7) focuses on the scope and purpose of research projects; at the middle school level, it asks students to engage in short research projects to answer a question about a significant topic, problem, or issue. While 6th and 7th grade students are expected to be able to respond to questions posed by the teacher, 7th grade students are also asked to begin generating additional related questions as they conduct their research, and 8th grade students are asked to generate their own initial and subsequent questions to frame the scope and purpose of their research.

Writing Standard 8 (W.8) addresses gathering and searching for information, as well as synthesizing that information in writing. In the elementary grades, this involves gathering information from print and digital sources and from personal experiences. In middle school, students gather information from multiple, credible sources. They must develop the ability to assess the credibility of their sources, a skill that is increasingly vital given the increase in unverified content available over the Internet. By 7th grade, students are expected to have mastered using search terms in library and online databases. In elementary school, students practiced paraphrasing and summarizing researched information, and they continue to extend these skills in middle school, as they focus on the proper way to quote material and how to avoid plagiarism and cite sources. By 7th grade, students should be able to provide in-text citations and bibliographies in a standard format, such as MLA or APA.

The final standard under the Research to Build and Present Knowledge heading, Writing Standard 9 (W.9), addresses the use of analytical reading skills to draw evidence from texts. This standard demonstrates how research activities connect to both reading and writing. Students must apply reading skills as they review research sources. They must analyze and compare information in the texts that they gather for research. The reference to reading in the standard underlines the fact that drawing evidence from texts is not only central to the reading standards but also a key aspect of research. Writing Standard 9 is uniform across the middle and high school grades, though the references to the reading standards change to reflect the particular standards for each grade level.

Range of Writing

For a lesson addressing Writing Standard 10 at the 6th grade level (W.6.10), see **Sample Lesson 1.**

The writing standards conclude with a single standard focused on the variety of writing tasks in which students should engage. Writing Standard 10, which is phrased exactly the same across the grade levels, is shown in Figure 3.6.

To meet this standard, students need opportunities to write routinely. Writing assignments should be a regular part of classroom activities and should include both extended writing that is improved after reflection and multiple drafts and focused writing tasks that take place in short time frames. Short writing assignments might, for example, ask students to respond to text-dependent questions or to reflect on a particular aspect of an oral or written text. Both consortia developing assessments for the Common Core are including a mix of short and long writing tasks; thus, students need to be able to produce a high-quality first draft under a tight deadline and to review and improve their writing through revision processes. Because student writing should address a variety of tasks, purposes, and audiences, students will need multiple opportunities to practice various writing types and forms. Teachers should design writing activities and assignments with a wide range of authentic purposes and audiences in mind.

W.10

Figure 3.6 | **Writing Standard 10: Range of Writing**

Grade 6 Students:	Grade 7 Students:	Grade 8 Students:
W.10 Write routinely over extended time frames (time for research, reflection, and revision) and shorter time frames (a single sitting or a day or two) for a range of tasks, purposes, and audiences.	**W.10** Write routinely over extended time frames (time for research, reflection, and revision) and shorter time frames (a single sitting or a day or two) for a range of tasks, purposes, and audiences.	**W.10** Write routinely over extended time frames (time for research, reflection, and revision) and shorter time frames (a single sitting or a day or two) for a range of tasks, purposes, and audiences.

CHAPTER 4

Speaking and Listening

Analyzing spoken messages, communicating with a variety of audiences, and integrating oral, visual, and graphic information are the key skills in the Common Core's Speaking and Listening strand. Although these skills are frequently evaluated in classroom and local assessments, they have not traditionally been included in high-stakes tests. At the time of this writing, both consortia developing assessments for the Common Core plan to include speaking and listening components. As teachers are likely unaccustomed to formal speaking and listening assessments, and because the approaches taken by the consortia differ, the details are worth examining here.

The Partnership for Assessment of Readiness for College and Careers is developing performance-based items to assess oral communication skills, which will be associated with research tasks. PARCC's speaking assessment will be required and will be scored locally by teachers, but it will not be part of students' final summative score (PARCC, 2010). In contrast, the Smarter Balanced Assessment Consortium, according to its draft content specifications for ELA assessments (Hess, 2011), plans to develop short summative speaking assessments that ask students to respond to a prompt. These responses will be recorded and scored externally. Other SBAC assessments will address oral presentation and collaborative discussion skills in connection with investigations or research tasks and will be scored locally by teachers. SBAC's current design calls for scores from these classroom assessments to be "certified" at the district level and reported to the state; recorded student performances will be audited to ensure consistent scoring. SBAC also plans to develop computer-based items to assess student listening skills for nonprint texts.

The standards in the Speaking and Listening strand (SL) are grouped under two headings: Comprehension and Collaboration, and Presentation of Knowledge and Ideas. We'll review each group in turn. It is important to note that, according to the Common Core State Standard Initiative's *Application to Students with Disabilities* (2010b), speaking and listening standards may be applied to the use of sign language for students requiring adaptations.

Comprehension and Collaboration

The first standard under this heading is Speaking and Listening Standard 1 (SL.1), which focuses on discussion skills and describes a variety of ways that students learn from each other during thoughtful academic conversations. This standard (see Figure 4.1) supports collaborative learning strategies and encourages teachers to support student learning by creating a variety of opportunities for students to discuss the material they are reading or researching. The components within Standard SL.1 describe specific skills that will support successful student collaboration; the detailed statements relate to focusing discussion ideas, effectively working with others, asking and answering questions, and synthesizing the discussion.

Students should have opportunities to engage in varied types of discussions and group work. By the time they reach middle school age, they are increasingly capable of conducting and monitoring effective group work on both a small scale and a larger one.

As compared to elementary school students, students in middle school are expected to use textual evidence to ground more of their discussions, comments, and questions and to refer to specifics in the material they study. Thus, discussion questions provided by teachers should ask students to support their ideas with evidence and sources. Standard SL.1 also

Figure 4.1 | **Speaking and Listening Standard 1: Comprehension and Collaboration—Discussion**

Grade 6 Students:	Grade 7 Students:	Grade 8 Students:
SL.1 Engage effectively in a range of collaborative discussions (one-on-one, in groups, and teacher-led) with diverse partners on *grade 6 topics, texts,* ***and issues,*** building on others' ideas and expressing their own clearly.	**SL.1** Engage effectively in a range of collaborative discussions (one-on-one, in groups, and teacher-led) with diverse partners on *grade 7 topics, texts, and issues,* building on others' ideas and expressing their own clearly.	**SL.1** Engage effectively in a range of collaborative discussions (one-on-one, in groups, and teacher-led) with diverse partners on ***grade 8*** *topics, texts, and issues,* building on others' ideas and expressing their own clearly.
a. Come to discussions prepared, having read or studied required material; explicitly draw on that preparation **by referring to evidence on the topic, text, or issue to probe and reflect on ideas under discussion.**	a. Come to discussions prepared, having read **or researched** material under study; explicitly draw on that preparation by referring to evidence on the topic, text, or issue to probe and reflect on ideas under discussion.	a. Come to discussions prepared, having read or researched material under study; explicitly draw on that preparation by referring to evidence on the topic, text, or issue to probe and reflect on ideas under discussion.
b. Follow rules for **collegial** discussions, **set specific goals and deadlines, and define individual roles as needed.**	b. Follow rules for collegial discussions, **track progress toward** specific goals and deadlines, and define individual roles as needed.	b. Follow rules for collegial discussions **and decision-making,** track progress toward specific goals and deadlines, and define individual roles as needed.
c. Pose and respond to specific questions **with elaboration and detail** by making comments that contribute to **the topic, text, or issue** under discussion.	c. Pose questions **that elicit elaboration** and respond **to others' questions and comments with relevant observations and ideas that bring the discussion back on topic as needed.**	c. Pose questions **that connect the ideas of several speakers** and elicit elaboration, and respond to others' questions and comments with relevant **evidence,** observations, and ideas.
d. Review the key ideas expressed and **demonstrate understanding of multiple perspectives through reflection and paraphrasing.**	d. **Acknowledge new information expressed by others and, when warranted, modify their own views.**	d. Acknowledge new information expressed by others, and, when warranted, **qualify or justify their own views and understanding in light of the evidence presented.**

Note: Boldface text identifies content that differs from the prior grade level.

focuses on growing students' ability to work collaboratively in a group. In the elementary grades, students are assigned roles within a group, but 6th grade students define and assign roles themselves when needed. Beginning in 6th grade, students set goals and deadlines, and as they progress through middle school, they track their own progress and learn to make collective decisions. Finally, middle school students are expected to be able summarize various perspectives from a discussion and refine their own ideas based on the ideas expressed by others.

The second and third standards under the Comprehension and Collaboration heading, Speaking and Listening Standards 2 and 3 (SL.2 and SL.3), focus on listening skills. SL.2 addresses evaluating information from various media, and SL.3 is about evaluating information from a speaker (see Figure 4.2).

SL.2–3

Figure 4.2 | **Speaking and Listening Standards 2–3: Comprehension and Collaboration—Listening**

Grade 6 Students:	Grade 7 Students:	Grade 8 Students:
SL.2 Interpret information presented in diverse media and formats (e.g., visually, quantitatively, orally) and **explain how it contributes to a topic, text, or issue under study.**	**SL.2 Analyze the main ideas and supporting details** presented in diverse media and formats (e.g., visually, quantitatively, orally) and explain how **the ideas clarify** a topic, text, or issue under study.	**SL.2 Analyze the purpose of** information presented in diverse media and formats (e.g., visually, quantitatively, orally) and **evaluate the motives (e.g., social, commercial, political) behind its presentation.**
SL.3 Delineate a speaker's argument and specific claims, distinguishing claims that are supported by reasons and evidence from claims that are not.	**SL.3** Delineate a speaker's argument and specific claims, **evaluating the soundness of the reasoning and the relevance and sufficiency of the evidence.**	**SL.3** Delineate a speaker's argument and specific claims, evaluating the soundness of the reasoning and relevance and sufficiency of the evidence **and identifying when irrelevant evidence is introduced.**

Note: Boldface text identifies content that differs from the prior grade level.

In elementary school, these two listening-focused standards require students to comprehend and summarize media and spoken messages, including quantitative formats such as graphs and charts. In middle school, these standards require more analysis from students. Speaking and Listening Standard 2 asks 6th grade students not only to understand the media that they see and hear but also to interpret its meaning by explaining how it relates to larger ideas and other texts. In 7th grade, students focus on analyzing the clarity of media information, and in grade 8, they focus on analyzing the purpose and motives behind spoken and visual texts. Although these standards concentrate on analyzing *the information* in media sources, they do not include analyzing *visual and oral techniques* used in media; those skills are addressed in the Reading Standards for Informational Text—specifically in RI.8 (see p. 25).

For a lesson addressing Speaking and Listening Standard 2 at the 6th grade level (SL.6.2), see **Sample Lesson 1**; to see the same standard addressed at the 8th grade level (SL.8.2), see **Sample Lesson 3**.

Speaking and Listening Standard 3 focuses on evaluating the logic and reasoning in spoken messages. Relatively uniform across the middle school grade levels, it applies to a variety of oral texts, including demonstrations and lectures, and it is a useful complement to RI.8 at grades 6, 7, and 8. In both the reading and the speaking and listening standards, students distinguish supported claims from unsupported claims in grade 6, evaluate the quality and adequacy of logic and reasoning in grade 7, and recognize when irrelevant evidence is introduced in grade 8.

Presentation of Knowledge and Ideas

As its name implies, the second heading in the Speaking and Listening strand covers standards focused on oral presentation skills. They ask students to present appropriate information clearly, use multimedia, and make appropriate language choices. Figure 4.3 shows the sequence of these standards across grade levels.

Speaking and Listening Standard 4 (SL.4) focuses on the content, organization, and delivery of student presentations. By the middle school

SL.4–6

Figure 4.3 | **Speaking and Listening Standards 4–6: Presentation of Knowledge and Ideas**		
Grade 6 Students:	Grade 7 Students:	Grade 8 Students:
SL.4 Present claims and findings, sequencing ideas logically and using **pertinent descriptions,** facts, and details **to accentuate main ideas or themes; use appropriate eye contact, adequate volume, and clear pronunciation.**	**SL.4** Present claims and findings, **emphasizing salient points in a focused, coherent manner** with pertinent descriptions, facts, details, and examples; use appropriate eye contact, adequate volume, and clear pronunciation.	**SL.4** Present claims and findings, emphasizing salient points in a focused, coherent manner with **relevant evidence, sound valid reasoning, and well-chosen** details; use appropriate eye contact, adequate volume, and clear pronunciation.
SL.5 Include multimedia components (e.g., graphics, **images, music,** sound) and visual displays in presentations **to clarify information.**	**SL.5** Include multimedia components and visual displays in presentations to clarify **claims and findings and emphasize salient points.**	**SL.5 Integrate** multimedia and visual displays into presentations to clarify information, **strengthen claims and evidence, and add interest.**
SL.6 Adapt speech to a variety of contexts and tasks, **demonstrating command** of formal English **when indicated** or appropriate.	**SL.6** Adapt speech to a variety of contexts and tasks, demonstrating command of formal English when indicated or appropriate.	**SL.6** Adapt speech to a variety of contexts and tasks, demonstrating command of formal English when indicated or appropriate.

Note: Boldface text identifies content that differs from the prior grade level.

years, students need to be able to orally communicate increasingly complex information and ideas, which means they need to become more selective when choosing supporting details to ensure that their presentation is focused and organized in a coherent manner that guides the listener. In elementary school, students practice speaking clearly and at an understandable pace. Work on oral delivery continues in middle school, where it expands to include using eye contact, appropriate volume, and proper pronunciation. By the time students leave middle school, they should have mastered these presentation skills and have a good foundation for SL.4's high school focus, which is adapting presentations for varying audiences and purposes.

Speaking and Listening Standard 5 (SL.5) focuses on the formats students use to present information or ideas. It places special emphasis on using multimedia, such as presentation software, for various purposes. The primary difference in SL.5 across the middle school grades is the purpose that the media serves within a presentation. In 6th grade, the focus is using media to clarify information; in 7th grade, it is using media to emphasize major points; and in 8th grade, the focus is using media to strengthen the presentation's overall argument and effectively engage the audience.

The final standard under the Presentation of Knowledge and Ideas heading, Speaking and Listening Standard 6 (SL.6), concerns the language students use when speaking. For presentations at the middle school level, students need to be able to select words and use a tone that is appropriate to various situations and audiences. For example, students will need to recognize that some contexts, such as expository academic presentations, call for a formal tone and adherence to correct grammatical conventions, per the Common Core language standards (see Chapter 5), whereas other purposes and contexts, such as working in collaborative groups with peers, call for less formality. For students to achieve SL.6, they must have a variety of opportunities to address different types of audiences and engage in a range of collaborative tasks. Furthermore, they should be prompted to practice their speaking and listening skills as they work with a variety of topics and subjects. The SBAC has indicated that the stimuli for its listening and speaking tasks may come from any subject area or content discipline (Hess, 2011). Notably, there are no speaking and listening standards in the set of Common Core standards for literacy in history/ social studies, science, and technical subjects.

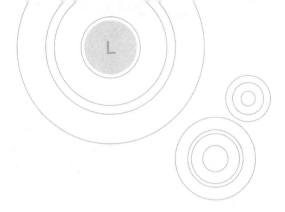

CHAPTER 5

Language

The Language strand (L) focuses on skills related to standard English grammar and usage, vocabulary, sentence fluency, and word choice. Because the skills in this strand support skills described in the Reading, Writing, and Speaking and Listening strands, they are easily addressed in conjunction with other Common Core standards in curricular units and daily lessons. The standards within the Language strand are organized under three headings: Conventions of Standard English, Knowledge of Language, and Vocabulary Acquisition and Use.

The consortia that are developing assessments for the Common Core will assess the language standards as part of constructed-response items and performance tasks that ask students to read, write, speak, and listen. For example, PARCC will assess students' ability to use correct English spelling and grammar as part of its performance-based assessment. However, both PARCC and SBAC are also likely to evaluate students' knowledge of English conventions and vocabulary skills within computer-scored, selected-response questions, such as multiple-choice items.

Conventions of Standard English

There are two standards for Conventions of Standard English. The first, Language Standard 1 (L.1), details grammar and usage conventions for both writing and speaking. The second, Language Standard 2 (L.2), lists specific rules related to capitalization, punctuation, and spelling in students' written work. The detailed components under each standard differ in each grade, with the exception being strategies related to spelling. While specific spelling strategies, such as word families and spelling patterns, are detailed in the standards for grades K–5, the standards for grades 6–12 simply ask students to correctly spell grade-appropriate words. Figure 5.1 shows the sequence of the Conventions of Standard English standards for students in grades 6, 7, and 8.

Figure 5.1 | **Language Standards 1–2: Conventions of Standard English**

Grade 6 Students:	Grade 7 Students:	Grade 8 Students:
L.1 Demonstrate command of the conventions of standard English grammar and usage when writing or speaking. a. **Ensure that pronouns are in the proper case (subjective, objective, possessive).** b. **Use intensive pronouns (e.g., myself, ourselves).** c. **Recognize and correct inappropriate shifts in pronoun number and person.** d. **Recognize and correct vague pronouns (i.e., ones with unclear or ambiguous antecedents).** e. **Recognize variations from standard English in their own and others' writing and speaking, and identify and use strategies to improve expression in conventional language.**	**L.1** Demonstrate command of the conventions of standard English grammar and usage when writing or speaking. a. **Explain the function of phrases and clauses in general and their function in specific sentences.** b. **Choose among simple, compound, complex, and compound-complex sentences to signal differing relationships among ideas.** c. **Place phrases and clauses within a sentence, recognizing and correcting misplaced and dangling modifiers.**	**L.1** Demonstrate command of the conventions of standard English grammar and usage when writing or speaking. a. **Explain the function of verbals (gerunds, participles, infinitives) in general and their function in particular sentences.** b. **Form and use verbs in the active and passive voice.** c. **Form and use verbs in the indicative, imperative, interrogative, conditional, and subjunctive mood.** d. **Recognize and correct inappropriate shifts in verb voice and mood.**

(continued)

L.1–2

Figure 5.1 | **Language Standards 1–2: Conventions of Standard English** *(continued)*

Grade 6 Students:	Grade 7 Students:	Grade 8 Students:
L.2 Demonstrate command of the conventions of standard English capitalization, punctuation, and spelling when writing. a. **Use punctuation (commas, parentheses, dashes) to set off nonrestrictive/ parenthetical elements.** b. Spell correctly.	**L.2** Demonstrate command of the conventions of standard English capitalization, punctuation, and spelling when writing. a. **Use a comma to separate coordinate adjectives (e.g., "It was a fascinating, enjoyable movie" but not "He wore an old[,] green shirt").** b. Spell correctly.	**L.2** Demonstrate command of the conventions of standard English capitalization, punctuation, and spelling when writing. a. **Use punctuation (comma, ellipsis, dash) to indicate a pause or break.** b. **Use an ellipsis to indicate an omission.** c. Spell correctly.

Note: Boldface text identifies content that differs from the prior grade level.

Language Standard 1 focuses on pronoun use in grade 6, on sentence structure in grade 7, and on verb use in grade 8. Note that all the skills addressed in these standards build on those acquired in earlier grades. For example, Language Standard 1 asks students to begin using simple verbs and pronouns correctly in grade 1, and the complexity of usage increases every year thereafter. In grade 3, L.1 stipulates that students understand the function of verbs and pronouns. With these types of progressions in place, by the end of 8th grade, students will have learned the majority of rules related to grammar and conventions. When they reach high school, they will be asked to apply those rules in increasingly complex writing and learn to manipulate sentences and language for diverse contexts.

Language Standard 2 builds students' knowledge of sentence structure by naming specific rules at each grade level for punctuating parenthetical elements, coordinating adjectives, asides, and omissions. Students are also expected to spell grade-level words correctly.

The specific grammar and convention rules listed in these standards are keyed to each grade level, which alerts teachers to the specific skills that should be their instructional focus. Both the body of the Common Core standards document and its Appendix A include a chart showing Language

Progressive Skills to provide further support. This chart identifies skills first introduced in lower grades that are likely to require continued attention in higher grades as students are challenged to apply these conventions to increasingly sophisticated forms of writing and speaking. A third of the skills listed in the Language Progressive Skills chart are introduced in 6th grade and continue to be developed throughout middle school. In addition to focusing on the conventions introduced in the standards at students' current grade level, middle school teachers should review the Language Progressive Skills chart to identify skills introduced at prior grade levels that they will need to revisit as students' writing and speaking become more sophisticated.

Because grammar and conventions are encountered in all literacy contexts, instruction and assessment focused on these skills have long been integrated into a wide variety of classroom activities. They are often addressed, for example, when students edit their own written assignments (editing is part of the writing process as defined in Writing Standard 5; see p. 40). The SBAC content specifications draft (Hess, 2012) indicates conventions may be assessed within a variety of reading, writing, and speaking tasks, as well as within focused editing tasks and items.

The Common Core standards do not dictate a change to the traditional approach of addressing conventions within the writing process; however, because very detailed skills are assigned to specific grades, teachers may need to provide direct instruction on the targeted skills for their grade level. The *PARCC Model Content Frameworks* (PARCC, 2011) notes that while grammar is meant to be a normal, everyday part of what students do, students should also be taught explicit lessons in grammar as they read, write, and speak.

Knowledge of Language

The Knowledge of Language heading covers only one standard, Language Standard (L.3), shown in Figure 5.2. This standard focuses on students' understanding of how language is selected and structured for different purposes and on their ability to apply this understanding when constructing or analyzing a text.

Figure 5.2 | **Language Standard 3: Knowledge of Language**

Grade 6 Students:	Grade 7 Students:	Grade 8 Students:
L.3 Use knowledge of language and its conventions when writing, speaking, reading, or listening. 　a. **Vary sentence patterns for meaning, reader/listener interest, and style.** 　b. **Maintain consistency in style and tone.**	**L.3** Use knowledge of language and its conventions when writing, speaking, reading, or listening. 　a. **Choose language that expresses ideas precisely and concisely, recognizing and eliminating wordiness and redundancy.**	**L.3** Use knowledge of language and its conventions when writing, speaking, reading, or listening. 　a. **Use verbs in the active and passive voice and in the conditional and subjunctive mood to achieve particular effects (e.g., emphasizing the actor or the action; expressing uncertainty or describing a state contrary to fact).**

Note: Boldface text identifies content that differs from the prior grade level.

In the elementary grades, students learned to select words, phrases, and sentence structures that convey their ideas in various formal and informal contexts. In middle school, students extend these skills by varying words, phrases, and sentence structures for more subtle effects, such as to stimulate reader interest and create a desired style and mood. Each grade has specific requirements for teachers to focus on, articulated within the components following the standard stem: grade 6 focuses on sentence patterns and consistency, grade 7 on eliminating wordiness, and grade 8 on passive and active voice. In high school, students will continue to work on these skills by evaluating the effects of such language choices on readers.

Vocabulary Acquisition and Use

As noted in Appendix A of the standards document, research supports vocabulary acquisition as a key element in student academic success, yet students' vocabulary acquisition tends to stagnate by grade 4 or 5. The three standards under the Vocabulary Acquisition and Use heading describe strategies for comprehending words and phrases encountered in texts, analysis of figurative meanings and word relationships, and the expansion of students' working vocabulary. Much of these standards' content is identical, not only across the middle school grades but also in the high school standards that follow them. That is not to say that student vocabulary skills are expected to stagnate—far from it. As the complexity of the texts that students encounter increases, so do the demands on students' working vocabulary. For example, students in grades 6–12 may apply the same essential strategies for vocabulary acquisition, but they apply these strategies to topics and texts that become more sophisticated from one grade level to the next. When designing lessons that address vocabulary, teachers should note that the content of Language Standards 4 and 5 (L.4 and L.5) and Reading Standard 4 (RL.4/RI.4) require the analysis of words and phrases in a text. Figure 5.3 shows the sequence of standards for the Vocabulary Acquisition and Use standards for middle school.

The first standard under this heading, Language Standard 4 (L.4), describes strategies for comprehending words and phrases found within oral or written texts. Students choose among vocabulary strategies, such as using context clues, derivations, and reference materials. Although the Common Core standards call for many of these skills to have been practiced in the elementary grades, the practice of verifying a word's meaning after an initial guess is not found before middle school, nor is the use of specialized reference materials.

For lessons addressing Language Standard 4 at all three middle school grades, see **Sample Lesson 1** (L.6.4), **Sample Lesson 2** (L.7.4), and **Sample Lesson 3** (L.8.4). Sample Lesson 3 also illustrates Language Standards 5 and 6 (L.8.4–5) at the 8th grade level.

Language Standard 5 (L.5) focuses on interpreting figures of speech and the relationships between words. The examples provided in the various statements of L.5 are specific to each grade level, helping to focus teachers' instruction and exposing students to a wide variety of figurative language and word relationships over the course of their schooling. Although students are introduced to synonyms in elementary school, for example, the concept of connotative meanings, or subtle associations among related words, does not appear in the standards until 6th grade. As students enter high school,

L.4–6

Figure 5.3 ǀ **Language Standards 4–6: Vocabulary Acquisition and Use**		
Grade 6 Students:	Grade 7 Students:	Grade 8 Students:

L.4 Determine or clarify the meaning of unknown and multiple-meaning words and phrases based on **grade 6** *reading and content,* choosing flexibly from a range of strategies.
   a. Use context (e.g., **the overall meaning of a sentence or paragraph; a word's position or function in a sentence**) as a clue to the meaning of a word or phrase.
   b. Use common, grade-appropriate Greek or Latin affixes and roots as clues to the meaning of a word (e.g., ***audience, auditory, audible***).
   c. Consult reference materials (e.g., dictionaries, glossaries, thesauruses), both print and digital, to find the pronunciation of a word or determine or clarify its precise meaning **or its part of speech.**
   d. **Verify the preliminary determination of the meaning of a word or phrase** (e.g., **by checking the inferred meaning in context or in a dictionary**).
	L.4 Determine or clarify the meaning of unknown and multiple-meaning words and phrases based on **grade 7** *reading and content,* choosing flexibly from a range of strategies.
	   a. Use context (e.g., the overall meaning of a sentence or paragraph; a word's position or function in a sentence) as a clue to the meaning of a word or phrase.
	   b. Use common, grade-appropriate Greek or Latin affixes and roots as clues to the meaning of a word (e.g., ***belligerent, bellicose, rebel***).
	   c. Consult **general and specialized** reference materials (e.g., dictionaries, glossaries, thesauruses), both print and digital, to find the pronunciation of a word or determine or clarify its precise meaning or its part of speech.
	   d. Verify the preliminary determination of the meaning of a word or phrase (e.g., by checking the inferred meaning in context or in a dictionary).
		L.4 Determine or clarify the meaning of unknown and multiple-meaning words or phrases based on **grade 8** *reading and content,* choosing flexibly from a range of strategies.
		   a. Use context (e.g., the overall meaning of a sentence or paragraph; a word's position or function in a sentence) as a clue to the meaning of a word or phrase.
		   b. Use common, grade-appropriate Greek or Latin affixes and roots as clues to the meaning of a word (e.g., ***precede, recede, secede***).
		   c. Consult general and specialized reference materials (e.g., dictionaries, glossaries, thesauruses), both print and digital, to find the pronunciation of a word or determine or clarify its precise meaning or its part of speech.
		   d. Verify the preliminary determination of the meaning of a word or phrase (e.g., by checking the inferred meaning in context or in a dictionary).

Figure 5.3 | **Language Standards 4–6: Vocabulary Acquisition and Use** *(continued)*   L.4–6

Grade 6 Students:	Grade 7 Students:	Grade 8 Students:

L.5 Demonstrate understanding of figurative language, word relationships, and nuances in word meanings.
    a. Interpret **figures of speech** (e.g., **personification**) in context.
    b. Use the relationship between particular words (e.g., **cause/effect, part/whole, item/category**) to better understand each of the words.
    c. **Distinguish among the connotations (associations) of words with similar denotations (definitions)** (e.g., *stingy, scrimping, economical, unwasteful, thrifty*).
	L.5 Demonstrate understanding of figurative language, word relationships, and nuances in word meanings.
	    a. Interpret figures of speech (e.g., **literary, biblical, and mythological allusions**) in context.
	    b. Use the relationship between particular words (e.g., **synonym/antonym, analogy**) to better understand each of the words.
	    c. Distinguish among the connotations (associations) of words with similar denotations (definitions) (e.g., *refined, respectful, polite, diplomatic, condescending*).
		L.5 Demonstrate understanding of figurative language, word relationships, and nuances in word meanings.
		    a. Interpret figures of speech (e.g., **verbal irony, puns**) in context.
		    b. Use the relationship between particular words to better understand each of the words.
		    c. Distinguish among the connotations (associations) of words with similar denotations (definitions) (e.g., *bullheaded, willful, firm, persistent, resolute*).

L.6 Acquire and use accurately *grade-appropriate* general academic and domain-specific words and phrases; **gather vocabulary knowledge when considering a word or phrase important to comprehension or expression.**	**L.6** Acquire and use accurately *grade-appropriate* general academic and domain-specific words and phrases; gather vocabulary knowledge when considering a word or phrase important to comprehension or expression.	**L.6** Acquire and use accurately *grade-appropriate* general academic and domain-specific words and phrases; gather vocabulary knowledge when considering a word or phrase important to comprehension or expression.

Note: Boldface text identifies content that differs from the prior grade level.

the emphasis of these standards changes so that students must consider how such expressions support the text as a whole. Overall, Language Standard 5 underlines the importance of students making connections to newly learned words in order to internalize the meaning of these words and understand the multiple ways that they can be used.

The final standard under Vocabulary Acquisition and Use, Language Standard 6 (L.6), addresses students' working vocabulary. As Appendix A describes, the Common Core standards emphasize academic vocabulary (words common across a variety of scholarly writings but rarely found in speech) and domain-specific words (words related to subject-area topics). When compared to the versions of this standard found in the elementary grades, the middle school statement of L.6 requires more self-directed pursuit of vocabulary and more independent application of strategies to unearth the meaning of unfamiliar words. However, teachers should still plan to expose students to academic and domain-specific words in multiple authentic contexts and to provide at least some direct vocabulary instruction, particularly on target words and particularly to struggling learners.

CHAPTER 6

Guidance for Instructional Planning

In this chapter, we provide a brief tutorial on designing lesson plans using the types of instructional strategies that appear in this guide's sample lessons. It includes a step-by-step outline for the development of lessons that make best use of proven instructional strategies and will help you ensure students master the new and challenging content represented by the Common Core standards.

The Framework for Instructional Planning

To identify and use effective strategies to develop these lessons, we draw on the instructional planning framework developed for *Classroom Instruction That Works, 2nd edition* (Dean et al., 2012), presented in Figure 6.1.

The Framework organizes nine categories of research-based strategies for increasing student achievement into three components. These components focus on three key aspects of teaching and learning: creating an environment for learning, helping students develop understanding, and helping students extend and apply knowledge. Let's take a close look at each.

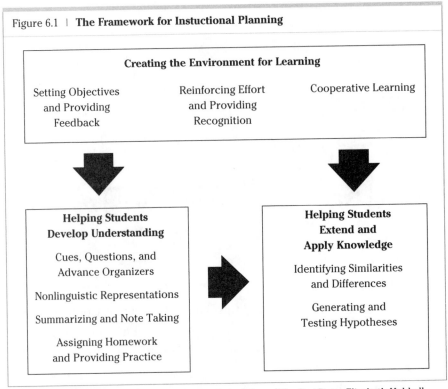

Figure 6.1 | **The Framework for Instuctional Planning**

Creating the Environment for Learning

Setting Objectives and Providing Feedback

Reinforcing Effort and Providing Recognition

Cooperative Learning

Helping Students Develop Understanding

Cues, Questions, and Advance Organizers

Nonlinguistic Representations

Summarizing and Note Taking

Assigning Homework and Providing Practice

Helping Students Extend and Apply Knowledge

Identifying Similarities and Differences

Generating and Testing Hypotheses

Source: From *Classroom Instruction That Works, 2nd ed.* (p. xvi) by Ceri Dean, Elizabeth Hubbell, Howard Pitler, and Bj Stone, 2012, Alexandria, VA: ASCD; and Denver, CO: McREL. Copyright 2012 by McREL. Adapted with permission.

Creating the environment for learning

Teachers create an environment for learning when they ensure that students are motivated and focused, know what's expected of them, and regularly receive feedback on their progress. When the environment is right, students are actively engaged in their learning and have multiple opportunities to share and discuss ideas with their peers.

A number of instructional strategies that help create a positive environment for learning may be incorporated into the lesson design itself. Other aspects, such as reinforcing effort and providing recognition, may not be a formal part of the lesson plan but are equally important. The following strategies are essential for creating a positive environment for learning:

- Setting objectives and providing feedback
- Reinforcing effort and providing recognition
- Cooperative learning

Helping students develop understanding

This component of the Framework focuses on strategies that are designed to help students work with what they already know and help them integrate new content with their prior understanding. To ensure that students study effectively outside class, teachers also need strategies that support constructive approaches to assigning homework. The strategies that help students develop understanding include the following:

- Cues, questions, and advance organizers
- Nonlinguistic representations
- Summarizing and note taking
- Assigning homework and providing practice

Helping students extend and apply knowledge

In this component of the Framework, teachers use strategies that prompt students to move beyond the "right answers," engage in more complex reasoning, and consider the real-world connections and applications of targeted content and skills, all of which help students gain flexibility when it comes to using what they have learned. The following strategies help students extend and apply knowledge:

- Identifying similarities and differences
- Generating and testing hypotheses

Figure 6.2 illustrates the three major components of teaching and learning described in *Classroom Instruction That Works,* along with the nine types, or categories, of strategies that further define the components and point

Figure 6.2 | Framework Components and the Associated Categories of Instuctional Strategies

Component	Category	Definition
Creating the Environment for Learning	Setting Objectives and Providing Feedback	Provide students with a direction for learning and with information about how well they are performing relative to a particular learning objective so they can improve their performance.
	Reinforcing Effort and Providing Recognition	Enhance students' understanding of the relationship between effort and achievement by addressing students' attitudes and beliefs about learning. Provide students with non-material tokens of recognition or praise for their accomplishments related to the attainment of a goal.
	Cooperative Learning	Provide students with opportunities to interact with one another in ways that enhance their learning.
Helping Students Develop Understanding	Cues, Questions, and Advance Organizers	Enhance students' ability to retrieve, use, and organize what they already know about a topic.
	Nonlinguistic Representations • Graphic Organizers • Pictures and Pictographs • Mental Images • Kinesthetic Movement • Models/Manipulatives	Enhance students' ability to represent and elaborate on knowledge using mental images.
	Summarizing and Note Taking	Enhance students' ability to synthesize information and organize it in a way that captures the main ideas and supporting details.
	Providing Practice, and Assigning Homework	Extend the learning opportunities for students to practice, review, and apply knowledge. Enhance students' ability to reach the expected level of proficiency for a skill or process

Component	Category	Definition
Figure 6.2 │ **Framework Components and the Associated Categories of Instuctional Strategies** *(continued)*		
Helping Students Extend and Apply Knowledge	Identifying Similarities and Differences • Comparing • Classifying • Creating/Using Metaphors • Creating/Using Analogies	Enhance students' understanding of and ability to use knowledge by engaging them in mental processes that involve identifying ways in which items are alike and different.
	Generating and Testing Hypotheses	Enhance students' understanding of and ability to use knowledge by engaging them in mental processes that involve making and testing hypotheses.

Source: From *Classroom Instruction That Works, 2nd ed.* (p. xviii) by Ceri Dean, Elizabeth Hubbell, Howard Pitler, and Bj Stone, 2012, Alexandria, VA: ASCD; and Denver, CO: McREL. Copyright 2012 by McREL. Adapted with permission.

you toward activities that will suit your learning objectives and support your students' success.

Lesson Development, Step by Step

To help you get started developing lessons that incorporate these strategies, we provide a step-by-step process by which you can ensure that you've had an opportunity to consider where within a lesson the various strategies might be used most effectively. Those steps are as follows:

1. Identify the focus for the lesson.
2. Determine how learning will be assessed.
3. Determine the activities that will start the lesson.
4. Determine the activities that will engage students in learning the content.
5. Determine the activities that will close the lesson.

Let's look now at the details of each step and how you might incorporate the nine effective instructional strategies associated with each of the

Framework's three components. We'll reference the sample lessons in this guide to illustrate particular aspects of this approach.

Step 1: Identify the focus for the lesson

The critical first step in crafting a lesson is to identify what students should learn as a result of their engagement in the lesson activities. Setting objectives for students also means establishing the guidelines for your development of the lesson: namely, that you will select and develop only those activities that will help students meet the objectives set. A learning objective is built directly from a standard; the objectives found in this guide's sample lessons are constructed from Common Core standards and listed under the heading "Common Core State Standards—Knowledge and Skills to Be Addressed."

Clarifying learning objectives. To ensure that students are clear about what they will learn, you will want your lesson plans to include more specific statements of the objectives in clear, student-friendly language. Some teachers accomplish this by using stems such as "I can . . ." or "We will be able to . . ." or "Students will be able to . . ." and providing a paraphrased version of the standard, simplifying the language as necessary. In the sample lessons for this guide, such specifics may be found under the headings "Knowledge/Vocabulary Objectives" and "Skill/Process Objectives" and prefaced by either "Students will understand . . ." or "Students will be able to. . . ."

Identifying essential questions and learning objectives. Framing the lesson's objectives under a broader essential question provides students with alternate avenues to find personal relevance and can energize them to seek answers as they begin a unit or lesson. The essential question properly focuses on the broader purpose of learning, and it is most effective when it is open-ended and not a question that can be easily answered. Each of the sample lessons includes an essential question—the learning objectives reframed to clarify for students what value the lesson holds for them.

Identifying foundational knowledge and possible misconceptions related to the learning objectives. As you develop learning objectives for a lesson, consider the other skills students will need to use but that will not be the explicit focus of instruction or assessment. Our discussions of each standard in this guide identify the critical knowledge and skills that students are assumed to have mastered or practiced in lessons prior to learning the new content. In the sample lessons, you'll find these standards under the heading "Common Core State Standards—Prior Knowledge and Skills to Be Applied."

Step 2: Determine how learning will be assessed

As important as identifying the learning objective for a lesson is identifying the criteria you will use to determine if students have met that objective. You will want to be clear about the rigor identified in the Common Core standards. As you develop scoring tools, such as checklists and rubrics that define the various levels of performance related to the objective's knowledge or skill, it is important to review the details of the objective's underlying standard to be sure you are looking for the appropriate level of mastery.

Assessing prior knowledge. Step 2 involves planning how to measure students' prior knowledge, especially the knowledge identified in Step 1 as prerequisite to mastery of the learning objective. For example, you might ask students to complete a short problem or share reflections on their prior experiences with similar tasks. This approach may also surface any lingering student misconceptions that you'll want to address before proceeding.

Providing feedback. This part of the planning process also includes deciding how you will provide students with feedback on their progress toward the outcome. Providing feedback is an important aspect of creating the environment for learning because understanding what good performance looks like, how to judge their own performance relative to a benchmark, and what they need to do to improve their performance helps students develop a sense of control over their learning. During lesson planning, you might also consider how peers can give their classmates feedback on progress toward the stated objective.

Step 3: Determine the activities that will start the lesson

Step 3 of the planning process concerns the activities at the start of the lesson related to the "Creating the Environment for Learning" component of the Framework for Instructional Planning. The beginning of each lesson should be orchestrated to capture students' interest, communicate the learning objectives, and encourage their commitment to effort.

Communicating learning objectives. You can share learning objectives by stating them orally, but be sure to post them in writing for reference throughout the lesson. Doing so not only reminds the class of the objectives' importance but also ensures that even students who weren't paying close attention or who came in late can identify what they are working to achieve.

Identifying the essential question and providing a context. Students engage in learning more readily when they can see how it connects to their own interests. The essential question you provide at the beginning of the lesson helps orient them to the purpose for learning. Students will also have a greater sense of involvement if you share with them what activities they'll be engaged in and how these activities will help build their understanding and skill. The sample lessons in this guide present this preview under the heading "Activity Description to Share with Students." It is something you might read aloud or post, along with the objectives and essential questions, as you create the environment for learning at the beginning of a lesson. To encourage greater involvement, you might also ask students to set personal goals based on the learning objectives in each activity. These personal goals may translate the learning objective to immediate goals that resonate for each student.

Reinforcing effort. As you develop the activities for the lesson, look for natural points where you might build in opportunities for students to receive encouragement they need to continue their work. To reinforce student effort, we need to help students understand the direct connection between how hard they work and what they achieve. It's another way in which teachers can provide students with a greater sense of control over their own learning.

Step 4: Determine the activities that will engage students in learning the content

At Step 4 we are at the crux of the lesson, deciding what students will do to acquire, extend, and apply knowledge or skills. This stage of planning includes identifying when formative assessment should take place, when you will provide students feedback from the assessment, and how you will ensure that students have a clear understanding of how they are doing. And, of course, you will need to decide which instructional activities will best serve the lesson's primary purposes, considering whether the activities need to focus on helping students acquire new knowledge and skill or extend and refine what they've already learned.

Choosing activities and strategies that develop student understanding. When your aim is to help students understand new information or a new process, then you will want to design activities that incorporate strategies associated with that component of the Framework for Instructional Planning. These are the strategies that help students access prior knowledge and organize new learning. Students come to every lesson with some prior knowledge, and the effective use of strategies such as using cues, questions, and advance organizers can enhance students' ability to retrieve and use what they already know about a topic in order to access something new. You can help students access and leverage their prior knowledge through simple discussion, by providing "KWL"-type advance organizers, by having students read or listen to short texts related to the targeted content, or any of a number of ways. Activities incorporating the use of nonlinguistic representations (including visualization) in which students elaborate on knowledge, skills, and processes are other good ways to help students integrate new learning into existing knowledge. The strategies of note taking and summarizing also support students' efforts to synthesize information through the act of organizing it in a way that captures its main ideas and supporting details or highlights key aspects of new processes. Finally, homework can help students learn or review new content and practice skills so that they can more quickly reach the expected level of proficiency. However, you will want to think carefully about your homework practices, as the research on what makes homework effective shows mixed results. Dean and colleagues (2012) recommend that teachers design homework assignments that directly support learning objectives. Students need to understand how homework serves lesson objectives, and once homework is completed, it is important that teachers provide feedback on the assignment.

Choosing activities and strategies that help students extend and apply knowledge. When your aim is to help students extend or apply their knowledge or master skills and processes, they will need opportunities to practice independently. What's beneficial are activities that involve making comparisons, classifying, and creating or using metaphors and analogies. Research summarized in the second edition of *Classroom Instruction That Works* indicates that these strategies, associated with the "Helping Students Extend and Apply Knowledge" component of the Framework for Instructional Planning, are a worthwhile use of instructional time. They help raise students' levels of understanding and improve their ability to use what they learn. Because students need to understand the concepts or skills that they're comparing, you are more likely to insert these activities later in a lesson than at the outset.

Remember, too, that strategies that help students generate and test hypotheses are not meant just for science classrooms. They are a way to deepen students' knowledge by requiring them to use critical-thinking skills, such as analysis and evaluation.

Grouping students for activities. Cooperative learning can be tremendously beneficial, whether students are developing an understanding of new knowledge or skill, or applying or extending it. With every lesson you design, consider when it makes sense to use this strategy, what kind of student grouping will be most beneficial, and how these groups should be composed. Cooperative learning is a strong option, for example, when you want to differentiate an activity based on student readiness, interest, or learning style. Consider, too, that students' learning experiences will be different depending on whether you permit them to self-select into groups of their choosing or assign their group partners, whether the groups are larger (four or five students) or smaller (e.g., pair work), and whether these groups are homogeneous or heterogeneous.

Providing students with the opportunity to share and discuss their ideas with one another in varying cooperative learning arrangements lays a foundation for the world beyond school, which depends on people working interdependently to solve problems and to innovate. Interacting with one another also deepens students' knowledge of the concepts they are learning; in other words, talking about ideas and listening to others' ideas helps students understand a topic and retain what they've learned, and it may send their thinking in interesting new directions.

Step 5: Determine the activities that will close the lesson

Bringing the lesson to a close provides an opportunity for you and students to look back on and sum up the learning experience.

During this part of the lesson, you want to return to the learning objectives and confirm that you have addressed each of them. This can be approached in one or more ways—through informal sharing, formative assessment, or even summative assessment. Students benefit from the opportunity to gauge their progress in learning. You might prompt them to reflect on the lesson in a journal entry, learning log, or response card, which can easily serve as an informal check for understanding. Note that asking students to share what they found most difficult as well as what worked well can provide you with insight you can apply during the next lesson and can use to refine the lesson just completed.

Depending upon the nature of the objective and whether the lesson appears late in the unit, you may elect to conduct a formal summative assessment. Alternatively, you may identify a homework assignment tied to the learning objective, making sure that students understand how the assignment will help them deepen their understanding or develop their skill.

* * *

In the remaining pages of this guide, we offer sample lesson plans based on the Common Core State Standards for English Language Arts, the Framework for Instructional Planning, and the steps just outlined.

Reading, Listening, and Seeing to Understand Poetry

Grade Level/Course: ELA grade 6
Length of Lesson: Two hours; two 60-minute class periods

Introduction

The Common Core State Standards emphasize the use of complex texts, one of which, Henry Wadsworth Longfellow's 1861 poem "Paul Revere's Ride" (identified in Appendix B as an exemplar for the grades 6–8 text complexity band), is explored in this lesson. Longfellow's use of robust vocabulary and complicated sentence structures to tell a compelling story based on historical events makes this poem a good complex text choice.

Over the course of two class periods, students work collaboratively to read Longfellow's narrative poem and define associated vocabulary terms. On their own, they compare and contrast two different ways of experiencing the poem. Please note that one of the suggested performance tasks provided in the standards' Appendix B concerns this poem (CCSSI, 2010e, p. 89). Although the multimedia material in this lesson is different from the material suggested in Appendix B, this lesson incorporates a similar idea as the students' final writing assignment.

Because the Common Core integrates standards for technology with the standards for English language arts, it's important for students to use simple technology in everyday lessons. Even though technology is not this lesson's principal focus, it provides students the opportunity to view Internet videos and download and use electronic versions of graphic organizers for all of their work, as resources allow.

Strategies from the Framework for Instructional Planning

- *Creating the Environment for Learning:* The lesson's essential question ("How does experiencing a poem in different ways—through reading, hearing, and considering the images it conveys—deepen your understanding of it?") and learning objective (see p. 76) are central to the lesson's content and provide a clear focus. Students work with partners and in small groups to develop an understanding of the poem, comparing versions of a text from different media. The teacher gives feedback and reinforces students' effort throughout the lesson.
- *Helping Students Develop Understanding:* Several strategies are used to help students develop understanding of the poem. Nonlinguistic representations used include two graphic organizers and a dramatic reading accompanied by visual images. Students collaborate and summarize what they are reading, and the practice provided by homework on vocabulary development furthers their comprehension.
- *Helping Students Extend and Apply Knowledge:* The summative task of comparing and contrasting brings all of the work together. Students explain how the different experiences of reading and listening helped them understand the poem. In sharing their explanation and listening to others' explanations, they extend and apply their knowledge.

Common Core State Standards—Knowledge and Skills to Be Addressed

Strand/Domain: Reading—Literature

Heading: Integration of Knowledge and Ideas
RL.6.7 Compare and contrast the experience of reading a story, drama, or poem to listening to or viewing an audio, video, or live version of the text, including contrasting what they "see" and "hear" when reading the text to what they perceive when they listen or watch.

Strand: Language

Heading: Vocabulary Acquisition and Use

L.6.4 Determine or clarify the meaning of unknown and multiple-meaning words and phrases based on grade 6 reading and content, choosing flexibly from a range of strategies.

a. Use context (e.g., the overall meaning of a sentence or paragraph; a word's position or function in a sentence) as a clue to the meaning of a word or phrase.

d. Verify the preliminary determination of the meaning of a word or phrase (e.g., by checking the inferred meaning in context or in a dictionary).

Strand: Writing

Heading: Range of Writing

W.6.10 Write routinely over extended time frames (time for research, reflection, and revision) and shorter time frames (a single sitting or a day or two) for a range of discipline-specific tasks, purposes, and audiences.

Strand: Speaking and Listening

Heading: Comprehension and Collaboration

SL.6.2 Interpret information presented in diverse media and formats (e.g., visually, quantitatively, orally) and explain how it contributes to a topic, text, or issue under study.

Common Core State Standards—Prior Knowledge and Skills to Be Applied

Strand/Domain: Reading—Literature

Heading: Key Ideas and Details

RL.6.1 Cite evidence to support analysis of what the text says explicitly as well as inferences drawn from the text.

Strand: Speaking and Listening

Heading: Comprehension and Collaboration

SL.6.1 Engage effectively in a range of collaborative discussions (one-on-one, in groups, and teacher-led) with diverse partners on grade 6 topics, texts, and issues, building on others' ideas and expressing their own clearly.

Teacher's Lesson Summary

In this lesson, students watch a video about Paul Revere's famous ride at the out-set of the American Revolution in order to build knowledge about this historical event through a multimedia text. Next, they silently read the poem "Paul Revere's Ride" by Henry Wadsworth Longfellow. Guided by a structured graphic organizer, they take notes on what they "see" and "hear" and work with a partner to read the poem aloud, discuss unfamiliar words, and use various sources to track down the meaning of any words they don't understand, recording these clarified or corrected meanings in the organizer.

The second class session exposes students to another way of experiencing "Paul Revere's Ride": a dramatic reading accompanied by visual images. Once again using an organizer to guide their work, students go on to review what they initially "saw" and "heard" in each of the poem's stanzas and summarize what they now see and hear, after having experienced the poem in alternative formats. The lesson concludes with a formal compare-and-contrast exercise and with students' sum-marizing how the various ways of encountering the poem have changed their sense of what it means.

Essential Question: How does experiencing a poem in different ways—through read-ing, hearing, and considering the images it conveys—deepen your understanding of it?
Learning Objective: To compare and contrast what is "seen" and "heard" when reading a poem to what is perceived when listening to the poem and watching images; to determine the meaning of words; to interpret content from a video and apply it to understanding a poem; to write a summary about how each experience of "reading" a poem helps create a fuller understanding.

Knowledge/Vocabulary Objectives

At the conclusion of this lesson, students will

• Understand a variety of potentially new vocabulary words essential to under-standing and analyzing Longfellow's poem "Paul Revere's Ride."

Skill/Process Objectives

At the conclusion of this lesson, students will be able to

• Compare and contrast three experiences of learning a poem.

- Determine the meaning of unfamiliar words from context.
- Summarize different learning experiences.

Resources/Preparation Needed

- A 10-minute expository video on the ride of Paul Revere, such as *The Ride,* a documentary focused on a historic reenactment of the event, available on YouTube: www.youtube.com/watch?v=Q1El-guPeEo&feature=related
- A print or electronic graphic organizer containing the full text of Longfellow's "Paul Revere's Ride" and prompts to guide reading, reflection, and vocabulary development (see Figure A, p. 86), one per student
- A recorded dramatic reading of "Paul Revere's Ride" accompanied by a series of still images, such as presented in *The Midnight Ride of Paul Revere*, a video by c-david cotrill-hall, available on YouTube: www.youtube.com/watch?v=U4h UMQG3MI8
- A print or electronic comparison matrix with prompts to guide students' identification of similarities and differences and capture the culminating writing activity (see Figure B, p. 93), one per student

Activity Description to Share with Students

Reading, discussing, listening, and seeing . . . this lesson is all about engagement with literature and about using your skills and senses to understand a poem—Henry Wadsworth Longfellow's "Paul Revere's Ride."

Who is Longfellow? He was an important American poet who was born in 1807 and died in 1882. Who is Paul Revere? Paul Revere was an American patriot who lived in Boston, Massachusetts, in 1775 at the beginning of the American Revolutionary War—the war the Americans fought to gain freedom from Great Britain. In this lesson, you will learn about Paul Revere, hear the poem Longfellow wrote about Paul Revere and published in 1861, and think about the images Longfellow created in that poem. You will read the poem several ways—both on your own and with a partner—and also by listening and "seeing." With your partner, you will discuss the poem's vocabulary. Comparing and contrasting the experience of reading text with the experience of viewing a multimedia rendition of that text are important skills for both future classwork and life in general. So much written text is dramatized in other media, and you'll want to be able to understand and talk about how different ways of presenting and encountering content contribute to that content's overall effect and influence the way that people understand it.

Lesson Activity Sequence—Class #1

Start the Lesson

1. Have students write what they anticipate the differences might be between reading a poem and then hearing the poem read out loud with accompanying pictures. Ask them to turn to the person next to them and share their thoughts.
2. Post and discuss the lesson's essential question and the lesson's learning objectives. Both should remain visible throughout the lesson's two class sessions.
3. Give students an overview of the learning experiences they'll be engaging in throughout the lesson.

Engage Students in Learning the Content

1. Build students' knowledge of Paul Revere by having them access the 10-minute video *The Ride,* a reenactment of the historic event. Ask students to take notes they might use to help them understand the poem.
2. Distribute or have students access individual blank copies of the **Graphic Organizer for Reading, "Seeing," and "Hearing" the Poem** (see **Figure A,** p. 81), which includes the full text of "Paul Revere's Ride." Students will use this organizer to guide their reading of the poem and consolidate their reactions to it. Model for students how to use the graphic organizer to capture what they "see" and "hear" in each of the poem's stanzas, as illustrated in Figure A.
3. Assign partners for a collaborative reading activity, which incorporates Speaking and Listening Standard 1. Explain to students that they should read the poem out loud, alternating stanzas with their partner. After each stanza, they should note and discuss unfamiliar words, find definitions of unfamiliar words using a dictionary or online source, and record these definitions in their graphic organizers.
4. Circulate through the classroom, conducting informal formative assessment of students' progress and providing feedback, such as prompting students to look for context clues to word meanings.

Close the Lesson

1. As a whole class, compare and contrast the experience of reading the poem individually and reading it out loud with a partner. You might, for example, choose a stanza and have the students reflect on paper for one minute how the experiences were alike or different, and then ask for volunteers to share their reflections.
2. *Homework:* Have students finish determining the meanings of any words they did not get to in class.

Lesson Activity Sequence—Class #2

Start the Lesson

1. Open by reminding students of the lesson's learning objectives: To compare and contrast what they can see "see" and "hear" when reading a poem to what they perceive when they listen to the poem and watch images related to it; and to write a summary about how the different ways of experiencing the poem increase their understanding of it.

Engage Students in Learning the Content

1. Have students access and watch the YouTube video *The Midnight Ride of Paul Revere,* c-david cotrill-hall's dramatic reading of "Paul Revere's Ride" accompanied by a variety of visual images. Then ask them to replay the video, but this time, reading along silently from a printed copy of the poem rather than watching the images on-screen.
2. Explain to students that their next activity will be to work on their own to record on their graphic organizers what they "see" and "hear" after having watched the video and listened to the poem. Encourage them to watch the video a second time through before they begin their work, and note that the class will reconvene in a designated amount of time to discuss and debrief the activity.
3. While students work, circulate throughout the room to check in on individual progress, assessing how students are doing and giving them feedback. Remind students of the learning targets focused on comparing and contrasting the experiences to help them take effective notes.

4. Begin the whole-group discussion by asking a few volunteers to share what they saw and heard with the rest of the class. Then distribute or have students access the **Comparison Matrix for Experiencing the Poem** (see **Figure B,** p. 88), and model one compare statement (how the experiences of reading the poem and listening to it with visual images were the same in terms of what was "seen" and "heard") and one contrast statement (how the experiences differed in terms of what was "seen" and "heard"). Instruct students to choose at least five different places within the poem and write their own compare and contrast statements for the characteristics of "see" and "hear" on their copy of the matrix.

Close the Lesson

1. Ask students to explain in writing (on the space provided in the Comparison Matrix) how the two different experiences—reading the poem and listening to the poem with visual images—developed their understanding of the poem.
2. Group students into groups of four to discuss what they have written.
3. At the conclusion of class, ask students to hand in their matrices and summaries. A third class period might be devoted to draft summary revision, with the revised products serving as a final assessment of comparing and contrasting.

Additional Resources for This Lesson

The Poetry Out Loud website offers some interesting ideas for enrichment activities. The web address is www.poetryoutloud.org/poems-and-performance/watch-video#.UBu7ycfW3K0.mailto

Figure A | Graphic Organizer for Reading, "Seeing," and "Hearing" the Poem

Stanza	"Paul Revere's Ride" (1861) by Henry Wadsworth Longfellow	Vocabulary	What Do You See and Hear?
1	Listen my children and you shall hear Of the midnight ride of Paul Revere, On the eighteenth of April, in Seventy-five; Hardly a man is now alive Who remembers that famous day and year.	in Seventy-five	Day 1—Reading the poem silently *Someone is telling the story of Paul Revere.* Day 1—Reading the poem aloud with a partner *Maybe the person telling the story was alive at the time—he might be a grandfather talking to his grandchildren about something that happened when he was a child a long time ago.* Day 2—Watching and hearing the poem *The words midnight and ride jumped out at me when I saw the picture that went with the words. You can see that it is dark and that a man is riding a horse all by himself through the streets.*
2	He said to his friend, "If the British march By land or sea from the town to-night, Hang a lantern aloft in the belfry arch Of the North Church tower as a signal light,— One if by land, and two if by sea; And I on the opposite shore will be, Ready to ride and spread the alarm Through every Middlesex village and farm, For the country folk to be up and to arm."	lantern aloft belfry to arm	Day 1—Reading the poem silently Day 1—Reading the poem aloud with a partner Day 2—Watching and hearing the poem

Note: Italicized text indicates a teacher-modeled response.

(continued)

Figure A | **Graphic Organizer for Reading, "Seeing," and "Hearing" the Poem** (*continued*)

Stanza	"Paul Revere's Ride" (1861) by Henry Wadsworth Longfellow	Vocabulary	What Do You See and Hear?
3	Then he said "Good-night!" and with muffled oar Silently rowed to the Charlestown shore, Just as the moon rose over the bay, Where swinging wide at her moorings lay The Somerset, British man-of-war; A phantom ship, with each mast and spar Across the moon like a prison bar, And a huge black hulk, that was magnified By its own reflection in the tide.	muffled oar moorings mast spar hulk	Day 1—Reading the poem silently Day 1—Reading the poem aloud with a partner Day 2—Watching and hearing the poem
4	Meanwhile, his friend through alley and street Wanders and watches, with eager ears, Till in the silence around him he hears The muster of men at the barrack door, The sound of arms, and the tramp of feet, And the measured tread of the grenadiers, Marching down to their boats on the shore.	eager ears muster barrack measured tread grenadiers	Day 1—Reading the poem silently Day 1—Reading the poem aloud with a partner Day 2—Watching and hearing the poem

| 5 | Then he climbed the tower of the Old North Church,
By the wooden stairs, with stealthy tread,
To the belfry chamber overhead,
And startled the pigeons from their perch
On the sombre rafters, that round him made
Masses and moving shapes of shade,—
By the trembling ladder, steep and tall,
To the highest window in the wall,
Where he paused to listen and look down
A moment on the roofs of the town
And the moonlight flowing over all. | stealthy
sombre
rafters | Day 1—Reading the poem silently

Day 1—Reading the poem aloud with a partner

Day 2—Watching and hearing the poem |
| 6 | Beneath, in the churchyard, lay the dead,
In their night encampment on the hill,
Wrapped in silence so deep and still
That he could hear, like a sentinel's tread,
The watchful night-wind, as it went
Creeping along from tent to tent,
And seeming to whisper, "All is well!"
A moment only he feels the spell
Of the place and the hour, and the secret dread
Of the lonely belfry and the dead;
For suddenly all his thoughts are bent
On a shadowy something far away,
Where the river widens to meet the bay—
A line of black that bends and floats
On the rising tide like a bridge of boats. | encampment
sentinel
bay | Day 1—Reading the poem silently

Day 1—Reading the poem aloud with a partner

Day 2—Watching and hearing the poem |

(continued)

Figure A | Graphic Organizer for Reading, "Seeing," and "Hearing" the Poem (continued)

Stanza	"Paul Revere's Ride" (1861) by Henry Wadsworth Longfellow	Vocabulary	What Do You See and Hear?
7	Meanwhile, impatient to mount and ride, Booted and spurred, with a heavy stride On the opposite shore walked Paul Revere. Now he patted his horse's side, Now he gazed at the landscape far and near, Then, impetuous, stamped the earth, And turned and tightened his saddle girth; But mostly he watched with eager search The belfry tower of the Old North Church, As it rose above the graves on the hill, Lonely and spectral and sombre and still. And lo! as he looks, on the belfry's height A glimmer, and then a gleam of light! He springs to the saddle, the bridle he turns, But lingers and gazes, till full on his sight A second lamp in the belfry burns.	spurred impetuous girth spectral bridle	Day 1—Reading the poem silently Day 1—Reading the poem aloud with a partner Day 2—Watching and hearing the poem
8	A hurry of hoofs in a village street, A shape in the moonlight, a bulk in the dark, And beneath, from the pebbles, in passing, a spark Struck out by a steed flying fearless and fleet; That was all! And yet, through the gloom and the light, The fate of a nation was riding that night; And the spark struck out by that steed, in his flight, Kindled the land into flame with its heat. He has left the village and mounted the steep, And beneath him, tranquil and broad and deep, Is the Mystic, meeting the ocean tides; And under the alders that skirt its edge, Now soft on the sand, now loud on the ledge, Is heard the tramp of his steed as he rides.	pebbles steed fleet fate steep tranquil Mystic alders	Day 1—Reading the poem silently Day 1—Reading the poem aloud with a partner Day 2—Watching and hearing the poem

#	Poem	Words	Activities
9	It was twelve by the village clock When he crossed the bridge into Medford town. He heard the crowing of the cock, And the barking of the farmer's dog, And felt the damp of the river fog, That rises after the sun goes down.	damp	Day 1—Reading the poem silently Day 1—Reading the poem aloud with a partner Day 2—Watching and hearing the poem
10	It was one by the village clock, When he galloped into Lexington. He saw the gilded weathercock Swim in the moonlight as he passed, And the meeting-house windows, black and bare, Gaze at him with a spectral glare, As if they already stood aghast At the bloody work they would look upon.	gilded weathercock aghast	Day 1—Reading the poem silently Day 1—Reading the poem aloud with a partner Day 2—Watching and hearing the poem

(continued)

Figure A | **Graphic Organizer for Reading, "Seeing," and "Hearing" the Poem** (*continued*)

Stanza	"Paul Revere's Ride" (1861) by Henry Wadsworth Longfellow	Vocabulary	What Do You See and Hear?
11	It was two by the village clock, When he came to the bridge in Concord town. He heard the bleating of the flock, And the twitter of birds among the trees, And felt the breath of the morning breeze Blowing over the meadow brown. And one was safe and asleep in his bed Who at the bridge would be first to fall, Who that day would be lying dead, Pierced by a British musket ball.	bleating flock musket ball	Day 1—Reading the poem silently Day 1—Reading the poem aloud with a partner Day 2—Watching and hearing the poem
12	You know the rest. In the books you have read How the British Regulars fired and fled,— How the farmers gave them ball for ball, From behind each fence and farmyard wall, Chasing the redcoats down the lane, Then crossing the fields to emerge again Under the trees at the turn of the road, And only pausing to fire and load.	ball for ball fire and load	Day 1—Reading the poem silently Day 1—Reading the poem aloud with a partner Day 2—Watching and hearing the poem

| 13 | So through the night rode Paul Revere;
 And so through the night went his cry of alarm
 To every Middlesex village and farm,—
 A cry of defiance, and not of fear,
 A voice in the darkness, a knock at the door,
 And a word that shall echo for evermore!
 For, borne on the night-wind of the Past,
 Through all our history, to the last,
 In the hour of darkness and peril and need,
 The people will waken and listen to hear
 The hurrying hoof-beats of that steed,
 And the midnight message of Paul Revere. | defiance <br> evermore <br> borne <br> peril | Day 1—Reading the poem silently

 Day 1—Reading the poem aloud with a partner

 Day 2—Watching and hearing the poem |

Figure B | Comparison Matrix for Experiencing the Poem

Question	Reading the Poem / Listening to the Poem with Visual Images
What did you see?	Compare—how were the experiences alike?
	1. In both experiences, I pictured a man, the narrator, telling a story about Paul Revere.
	2.
	3.
	4.
	5.
	Contrast—how were the experiences different?
	1. After reading stanza one by myself, I didn't really see Paul Revere riding his horse. After listening to the poem, seeing the pictures, and reading along, I could see a man riding alone in the night in the streets of Boston. I could actually see the midnight ride. The two experiences were different.
	2.
	3.
	4.
	5.
What did you hear?	Compare—how were the experiences alike?
	1.
	2.
	3.
	4.
	5.
	Contrast—how were the experiences different?
	1.
	2.
	3.
	4.
	5.

Synthesis and Summary: Explain how each experience contributed to your understanding of the poem.

Note: Italicized text indicates a teacher-modeled response.

Exploring the Development of the Central Ideas in Churchill's "Blood, Toil, Tears and Sweat"

Grade Level/Course: ELA grade 7
Length of Lesson: Two hours; two 60-minute class periods

Introduction

The Common Core reading standards emphasize text analysis to the extent that "eighty to ninety percent of the Reading standards in each grade require text dependent analysis" (Coleman & Pimentel, 2012, p. 6). To address this emphasis, teachers might consider designing or reframing their lessons so that the majority of questions and reading activities require students to base their responses or analysis on specifics in the text. The standards also emphasize the reading of literary nonfiction, and, as stated in Reading Standard 10, students are expected to begin high school capable of reading this kind of text independently and proficiently. For these reasons, it is important for middle school teachers across the content areas to incorporate the reading and analysis of literary nonfiction into their curriculum, using texts at the appropriate level of complexity and providing scaffolding, as needed.

This lesson, built around Winston Churchill's "Blood, Toil, Tears and Sweat: Address to Parliament on May 13th, 1940" (identified in Appendix B of the standards document as a complex text appropriate for grades 6–8), asks 7th grade students to determine the meaning of words using clues in the text and to identify and describe how the author (Churchill) develops his central ideas, citing textual evidence to support their insights. Churchill's speech is rich in persuasive language, making it a good text for students beginning to build these skills.

Strategies from the Framework for Instructional Planning

- *Creating the Environment for Learning:* The lesson's essential question ("How do authors develop their central ideas?") and learning objective ("To determine the meaning of words using clues in the text and to cite evidence from the text to support an analysis of the development of central ideas in an historic speech") are central to the lesson's content and provide a clear focus. A variety of built-in supports, including teacher modeling of task completion, regular checks for understanding, and feedback, help students of varying reading proficiencies access what is a relatively complex text. Students engage in cooperative learning (collaborative partnerships/groups) during each of the lesson's two class sessions and also have opportunities for independent work.
- *Helping Students Develop Understanding:* The lesson features several strategies to help students integrate what they already know to build understanding, including the use of cues, questions, and advance organizers. The presentation of the text in audio format gives students a nonlinguistic representation of the material, and homework involving the use of a dictionary and online resource provides practice.
- *Helping Students Extend and Apply Knowledge:* The lesson's summative activity— citing evidence that supports the development of Churchill's central ideas— gives students the opportunity to apply what they have learned. They extend their knowledge further by sharing the hypothesis they've generated with one another and using one another's insights to refine understanding.

Common Core State Standards—Knowledge and Skills to Be Addressed

Strand: Language

Heading: Vocabulary Acquisition and Use

L.7.4 Determine or clarify the meaning of unknown and multiple-meaning words and phrases based on grade 7 reading and content, choosing flexibly from a range of strategies.

a. Use context (e.g., the overall meaning of a sentence or paragraph; a word's position or function in a sentence) as a clue to the meaning of a word or phrase.

d. Verify the preliminary determination of the meaning of a word or phrase (e.g., by checking the inferred meaning in context or in a dictionary).

Strand/Domain: Reading—Informational Text

Heading: Key Ideas and Details

RI.7.1 Cite several pieces of textual evidence to support analysis of what the text says explicitly as well as inferences drawn from the text.

RI.7.2 Determine two or more central ideas in a text and analyze their development over the course of the text; provide an objective summary of the text.

Heading: Range of Reading and Level of Text Complexity

RI.7.10 By the end of the year, read and comprehend literary nonfiction in the grades 6–8 text complexity band proficiently, with scaffolding as needed at the high end of the range.

Strand: Speaking and Listening

Heading: Comprehension and Collaboration

SL.7.2 Analyze the main ideas and supporting details presented in diverse media and formats (e.g., visually, quantitatively, orally) and explain how the ideas clarify a topic, text, or issue under study.

Common Core State Standards—Prior Knowledge and Skills to Be Applied

Strand: Speaking and Listening

Heading: Comprehension and Collaboration

SL.7.1 Engage effectively in a range of collaborative discussions (one-on-one, in groups, and teacher-led) with diverse partners on grade 7 topics, texts, and issues, building on others' ideas and expressing their own clearly.

a. Come to discussions prepared, having read or researched material under study; explicitly draw on that preparation by referring to evidence on the topic, text, or issue to probe and reflect on ideas under discussion.

Teacher's Lesson Summary

In this lesson, students listen to and read Winston Churchill's famous "Blood, Toil, Tears and Sweat: Address to Parliament on May 13th, 1940." Working in collaborative groups, students use context clues to develop their understanding of particular words in Churchill's address. Then, both independently and in collaborative groups, they cite evidence from the text that supports Churchill's central ideas: the legitimacy of his newly formed government and the issue of a national call to arms. The two class sessions described might be followed by a third session in which students create an objective summary of the speech (as described in Standard RI.7.2).

Essential Question: How do authors develop their main ideas?
Learning Objective: To determine the meaning of words using clues in the text; to cite evidence from the text to support an analysis of the development of central ideas in a historic speech.

Knowledge/Vocabulary Objectives

At the conclusion of this lesson, students will

- Understand the concept of a vote of confidence.
- Understand the concept of a call to arms.
- Understand a variety of potentially new vocabulary words and phrases necessary to comprehend Churchill's speech, uncover its main ideas, and analyze its content.

Skill/Process Objectives

At the conclusion of this lesson, students will be able to

- Determine the meaning of words in a text by using context clues.
- Cite evidence from a text to support its analysis.

Resources/Preparation Needed

1. An approximately 10-minute video documentary on the 1939 Invasion of Poland, such as *WWII 1st of September 1939 Invasion of Poland in Colour*, available on You Tube: (www.youtube.com/watch?v=bpYpbilZDGw&feature=related).

- An advance organizer to support collaborative and independent analysis of the vocabulary and phrases used in Churchill's "Blood, Toil, Tears and Sweat: Address to Parliament on May 13th, 1940" (see Figure A, p. 98), one per student
- Copies of the full text of "Blood, Toil, Tears and Sweat," one per student. An excerpt paragraph of this speech is provided on page 91 of Appendix B of the Common Core ELA standards document, and the full text is readily available online.
- An audio recording of "Blood, Toil, Tears and Sweat" (available: www.history place.com/speeches/churchill.htm)
- A graphic organizer for citing textual evidence (see Figure B, p. 100), one per student

Activity Description to Share with Students

"Blood, Toil, Tears and Sweat!" Who said that? What did the speaker mean?

In this lesson, you will listen to and read a famous speech that Winston Churchill made to the elected members of Parliament in May 1940. Then you will participate in a series of guided learning activities in which you and your classmates examine this speech carefully, gathering evidence to support your conclusions about the message Churchill intended to send. This particular speech marked a turning point in Great Britain's history. As you examine the text closely, you will read like a detective to figure out Churchill's intentions and then make a case for your interpretation.

Lesson Activity Sequence—Class #1

Start the Lesson

1. Post and discuss the lesson's essential question and learning objective. Both should remain posted throughout the lesson's two class sessions.
2. Give students an overview of the learning experiences they'll be engaging in throughout the lesson.
3. As an anticipatory set, ask students to write down what they know about the beginning of World War II and then take a minute to share what they wrote with a partner. Show a 10-minute video documentary of the German invasion of Poland to hook student interest, create lesson context, and build student knowledge about what was happening in Europe in the months leading up to Churchill's "Blood, Toil, Tears and Sweat" speech. After the video, have students write what

they now know about the early days of World War II. Ask them to share with a partner, and then call upon a few volunteers to share with the class.

4. Distribute the **Advance Organizer for Vocabulary Acquisition** (see **Figure A,** p. 98), and explain to students that it identifies a number of key terms in the speech they are about to read and listen to. Point out that they will need to pay particular attention to these words in the speech and note how Churchill uses them.

Engage Students in Learning the Content

1. Give students a printed copy of "Blood, Toil, Tears and Sweat," and ask them to read it. As they read, they should highlight both the words and phrases that are listed in the vocabulary handout and any other words or phrases they don't understand. As students work, walk around the room checking in with individuals and gathering informal data about their understandings.

2. Play a recording of Churchill's speech. As students listen and read along, have them note the highlighted words they will define from the context.

3. When the audio has finished playing, use the think-aloud strategy as you model for students how to use the vocabulary graphic organizer (see the example entry in Figure A).

4. Have students work in teacher-selected pairs to reread the speech, working collaboratively to identify contextual cues, infer the meaning of highlighted words, and then record these meanings in their individual graphic organizer. Give students a time limit for this work.

5. As students work, walk around the room, monitoring their progress and providing supportive feedback, directing the students to focus on context clues.

6. After a set amount of time, pair the partners with another pair, using your own selection process, and have them share their definitions with one another. They should discuss differences in their interpretations or new insights.

Close the Lesson

1. Distribute note cards, one per student, and ask everyone to write a short paragraph stating and reflecting on what they believe to be the main ideas in the "Blood, Toil, Tears and Sweat" speech. Collect and review these cards for evidence of what students learned in Class #1, and, if needed, adjust your plans for the next class session, based on this formative data.

2. *Homework:* Explain to students they will need to complete the final column of the vocabulary handout, looking up the definitions of the targeted words and phrases in a dictionary or online source to verify (or correct, as needed) the meanings they inferred from the context.

Lesson Activity Sequence—Class #2

Start the Lesson

1. Open by reviewing one of the posted learning objectives: cite evidence from the text to support an analysis of the development of central ideas of a speech.
2. Working as a whole class, review the homework for completion and accuracy. Create a whole-class organizer with input from volunteer students.

Engage Students in Learning the Content

1. Explain to students that now that they have a firmer grasp on the meaning of the specific words and phrases Churchill used in the "Blood, Toil, Tears and Sweat" address, they have the tools they need to identify the central ideas he was attempting to get across and to analyze how he chose to develop those ideas in his speech. Play the recording of Churchill's speech again, asking students to listen for the central ideas.
2. Redistribute the note cards students submitted at the close of the previous day's class, and ask them to reread what they wrote. Give them a few minutes to revise, delete information, or add to their thoughts about the central ideas in Churchill's speech. Have them share their revised ideas with the rest of the class.
3. Break the class into different teacher-designated pairs from Class #1, so students can work with new partners, and give the pairs a few minutes to hypothesize about the meaning of the phrases "vote of confidence" and "call to arms."
4. Distribute copies of the **Graphic Organizer for Citing Textual Evidence** (see **Figure B,** p. 100). Use the graphic organizer to model for students how to cite textual evidence from the speech to support the development of a central idea. For example, using the example provided, show students how to cite words and phrases that support Churchill's request for recognition of his formation of a new government. Then have students work independently to cite evidence for that central idea or another (e.g., his call to arms). After a short period of time

(10 minutes could be enough), call for a partner check-in—a time for students to share their ideas and insights with their partner and to give and receive feedback—before returning to independent work for another short period of time (15 minutes or so).

Close the Lesson

1. Organize students into small groups of three or four for another collaboration time, and give them a designated amount of time to share their insights with one other.
2. Finish with a whole-class sharing session. As individuals report out, use a whiteboard, SMART Board, or overhead to compile a class-generated list of central ideas and textual evidence, leading students in a reflection on and summary of how each piece of evidence supports the development of the speech's central ideas.

Additional Resources for This Lesson

There are a number of good online sources of information about Winston Churchill, "Blood, Toil, Tears and Sweat," and the events surrounding his rise to prime minister of Great Britain:

- www.bbc.co.uk/history/worldwars/wwtwo/churchill_defender_01.shtml
- www.historyplace.com/speeches/churchill.htm
- https://www.winstonchurchill.org/learn/speeches/speeches-of-winston-churchill/1940-finest-hour/92-blood-toil-tears-and-sweat

For an extension activity or further study, students can read, listen to, and analyze Franklin D. Roosevelt's speech "For a Declaration of War" and then compare its content and rhetoric to the content and rhetoric of Churchill's speech. Roosevelt's speech is available at www.historyplace.com/speeches/fdr-infamy.htm

Figure A	Advance Organizer for Vocabulary Acquisition		
Word or Phrase	**Context**	**Preliminary Inferred Meaning**	**HOMEWORK Corrected or Refined Meaning**
inflexible resolve	*". . . welcomes the formation of a government representing the united and inflexible resolve of the nation . . . "*	*the country wants the new government*	*Inflexible = not moving, not flexible* *Resolve = determination*
(I beg to) move			
Commission			
War Cabinet			
late Government			
Three Fighting Services			
Ministers			
Parliament			
His Majesty			
summoned			
Mr. Speaker			
Note: Italicized text indicates a teacher-modeled response.			

Figure A **Advance Organizer for Vocabulary Acquisition** *(continued)*			
Word or Phrase	**Context**	**Preliminary Inferred Meaning**	**HOMEWORK Corrected or Refined Meaning**
provision			
colleagues			
grievous			
policy			
tyranny			
surpassed			
lamentable			
buoyancy			

Figure B **Graphic Organizer for Citing Textual Evidence**		
Hypothesis: Central Idea	**Evidence:** Excerpted Text That Supports the Central Idea	**Explanation:** How the Text Supports the Central Idea
Why Churchill formed a new government	*"I received His Majesty's commission to form a new Administration" (paragraph 1, line 2)*	*The king asked him to form a new government.*
Note: Italicized text indicates a teacher-modeled response.		

Playing with Words

Grade Level/Course: ELA grade 8
Length of Lesson: Two hours; two 60-minute class periods

Introduction

Vocabulary development is a thread that runs throughout the Common Core English language arts standards and across its strands; students are asked to build word knowledge through reading, writing, speaking, and listening. Research shows that students benefit from direct instruction in vocabulary development, including the nuances of words and how words and phrases are used in text to develop meaning and tone. In addition, the standards stipulate that students should receive many opportunities to "use and respond to the words they learn through playful informal talk, discussion, reading or being read to, and responding to what is read" (CCSSI, 2010d, p. 32). In grade 8, "playful informal talk" fits well with students' analysis of literary devices in Ambrose Bierce's *The Devil's Dictionary* and Colin Bowles's *The Wit's Dictionary,* which are the teacher texts for this lesson.

Strategies from the Instructional Planning Framework

- *Creating the Environment for Learning:* In this lesson, the learning objectives (see p. 104) provide a clear frame for the development and application of student knowledge. Cooperative group work—including small-group work, partner work, and whole-class discussion—is employed to support "playful informal talk" about words. Feedback about and recognition of others' ideas flow through all of the activities as students talk about words.

- *Helping Students Develop Understanding:* Direct instruction is employed to build students' background knowledge about figures of speech and other literary devices authors use to convey meaning and tone. The use of cues, questions, and graphic organizers enhances students' ability to organize this new knowledge and to use it as they analyze definitions presented in "alternative dictionaries."
- *Helping Students Extend and Apply Knowledge:* Once students understand the literary devices and figures of speech presented, they extend and apply their new knowledge using words from their everyday lives (e.g., *middle school* or *Internet*) when they write their own definitions and determine figures of speech before presenting them to the class.

Common Core State Standards—Knowledge and Skills to Be Addressed

Strand: Language

Heading: Vocabulary Acquisition and Use

L.8.4 Determine or clarify the meaning of unknown and multiple-meaning words or phrases based on grade 8 reading and content, choosing flexibly from a range of strategies.

c. Consult general and specialized reference materials (e.g., dictionaries, glossaries, thesauruses), both print and digital, to find the pronunciation of a word or determine or clarify its precise meaning or its part of speech.

L.8.5 Demonstrate understanding of figurative language, word relationships, and nuances in word meanings.

a. Interpret figures of speech (e.g., verbal irony, puns) in context.

b. Use the relationship between particular words to better understand each of the words.

c. Distinguish among the connotations (associations) of words with similar denotations (definitions) (e.g., *bullheaded, willful, firm, persistent, resolute*).

L.8.6 Acquire and use accurately grade-appropriate general academic and domain-specific words and phrases; gather vocabulary knowledge when considering a word or phrase important to comprehension or expression.

Strand/Domain: Reading—Informational Text

Heading: Craft and Structure

RI.8.4 Determine the meaning of words and phrases as they are used in a text, including figurative, connotative, and technical meanings; analyze the impact of specific word choices on meaning and tone, including analogies or allusions to other texts.

Common Core State Standards—Prior Knowledge and Skills to Be Applied

Strand: Language

Heading: Conventions of Standard English

L.8.2 Demonstrate command of the conventions of standard English capitalization, punctuation, and spelling when writing.

a. Use punctuation (comma, ellipsis, dash) to indicate a pause or break.

c. Spell correctly.

Heading: Vocabulary Acquisition and Use

L.8.4 Determine or clarify the meaning of unknown and multiple-meaning words or phrases based on grade 8 reading and content, choosing flexibly from a range of strategies.

c. Consult general and specialized reference materials (e.g., dictionaries, glossaries, thesauruses), both print and digital, to find the pronunciation of a word or determine or clarify its precise meaning or its part of speech.

d. Verify the preliminary determination of the meaning of a word or phrase (e.g., by checking the inferred meaning in context or in a dictionary).

L.8.5 Demonstrate understanding of figurative language, word relationships, and nuances in word meanings.

b. Use the relationship between particular words to better understand each of the words.

Strand: Writing

Heading: Production and Distribution of Writing
W.8.4 Produce clear and coherent writing in which the development, organization, and style are appropriate to task, purpose, and audience.

Strand: Speaking and Listening

Heading: Comprehension and Collaboration
SL.8.1 Engage effectively in a range of collaborative discussions (one-on-one, in groups, and teacher-led) with diverse partners on grade 8 topics, texts, and issues, building on others' ideas and expressing their own clearly.

Heading: Presentation of Knowledge and Ideas
SL.8.4 Present claims and findings, emphasizing salient points in a focused, coherent manner with relevant evidence, sound valid reasoning, and well-chosen details; use appropriate eye contact, adequate volume, and clear pronunciation.

Teacher's Lesson Summary

In this lesson, you use direct instruction to build students' vocabulary knowledge about key literary terms: *connotation, denotation, hyperbole, metaphor, pun, sarcasm, sardonic tone, simile, tone, verbal irony,* and *wit*. Students use these words as they collaboratively analyze the meaning and tone of selected definitions of familiar and unfamiliar words found in two specialized dictionaries. (The authors of these texts definitely play with words!) Students present their analysis of the definitions they study. Then they write and have the opportunity to present their own "playing with words" definitions.

Essential Question: How can unusual word definitions evoke meaning and tone?
Learning Objective: To learn how authors use figures of speech and tone to convey meaning.

Knowledge/Vocabulary Objectives

At the conclusion of this lesson, students will

- Understand the meaning of the terms *connotation, denotation, hyperbole, metaphor, pun, sarcasm, sardonic tone, simile, tone, verbal irony,* and *wit.*
- Understand how word choice changes the meaning and tone of writing.

Skill/Process Objectives

At the conclusion of this lesson, students will be able to

- Recognize figures of speech, such as hyperbole, metaphor, pun, and simile in text.
- Identify an author's intent or tone, such as irony, sarcasm, sardonic tone, and wit in text.
- Use figures of speech and convey tone in their own writing.

Resources/Preparation Needed

- Ambrose Bierce's *The Devil's Dictionary* (in the public domain and available at www.thedevilsdictionary.com/) and Colin Bowles's *The Wit's Dictionary* (Kindle version available from amazon.com)
- Background information on Ambrose Bierce (www.online-literature.com/bierce/ and www.biercephile.com)
- The online *Merriam-Webster Dictionary* (www.m-w.com/)
- A prepared advance organizer for vocabulary self-assessment and development (see Figure A, p. 110), one per student
- A prepared graphic organizer for definition analysis (see Figure B, p. 111), one per student
- A prepared set of guidelines for the application activity—creating and discussing "playful" definitions of familiar words (see Figure C, p. 115)

Activity Description to Share with Students

A dictionary is a dictionary, right? They're all the same: words presented alphabetically and then defined. All very cut and dried; all very serious. In this lesson, you'll see that this is not necessarily the case at all.

Ambrose Bierce was an early 20th century American journalist and writer who wrote his own "word book," later known as *The Devil's Dictionary*. You will look at this text and see how Bierce uses words cleverly to create distinct meaning and tone in dictionary definitions. His work inspired others, including Colin Bowles, to write their own dictionaries. You may find yourself smiling or even laughing out loud as you analyze how these authors play with words. After you've taken a look at their alternative definitions of familiar words, you'll have the opportunity to play with words in the way that they do. You will use the literary devices and figures of speech we will be looking at in this lesson to write your own alternative definitions, conveying your own individual meaning and tone.

Lesson Activity Sequence—Class #1

Start the Lesson

1. Post and discuss the essential question: How can unusual word definitions evoke meaning and tone?
2. Post and discuss the learning objectives: To learn literary terms, analyze unusual dictionary definitions for meaning and tone, and apply key literary terms to the special definitions.
3. Give students a quick overview of the activities they'll be engaging in.
4. Give every student a copy of the **Advance Organizer for Vocabulary Assessment and Development: Literary Terminology** (see **Figure A**, p. 110), which functions as a pre-assessment and a way for students to access their prior knowledge. Give students a set amount of time to rate how well they know the key literary terms that will be the focus of the lesson. Cueing students in this fashion will help them organize the new knowledge they will encounter.
5. Explain the definitions, or denotations, of the terms listed in the organizer, using the Merriam-Webster online dictionary (www.merriam-webster.com/dictionary) as your source. Ask students to write definitions of these words on their organizer, based on the explanations you provide.

Stress to students that these definitions will serve as the baseline when they are analyzing definitions during the next activity.

Engage Students in Learning the Content

1. Give the students a little background on the authors of *The Devil's Dictionary* and *The Wit's Dictionary* (see "Activity Description to Share with Students").
2. Distribute copies of the **Graphic Organizer for Definition Analysis** (see **Figure B,** p. 111), and then use a prepared and projected version of the handout to model the class session's main activity: looking at definitions from two of the three dictionaries (one a denotation from Merriam-Webster and the other an "alternate definition" from Bierce or Bowles) and analyzing the "playful" definitions for their figures of speech, meaning, and tone. Here is an example, using Bierce's definition of the word *dictionary:*

Definition from Merriam-Webster's Online Dictionary* (denotation)	Bierce's definition:	Which figure(s) of speech does the alternative definition use?	What point is the author making, and how does he employ the identified figure of speech?	What is the author's tone?
DICTIONARY, n. a reference source in print or electronic form containing words usually alphabetically arranged along with information about their forms, pronunciations, functions, etymologies, meanings, and syntactical and idiomatic uses	*DICTIONARY, n.* A malevolent literary device for cramping the growth of a language and making it hard and inelastic. This dictionary (*The Devil's Dictionary*), however, is a most useful work.	Verbal irony	*He thinks a dictionary is a wicked tool that limits language. He thinks the denotation—the literal meaning, of the word dictionary—stops language from growing, because the definitions are set, rigid. He believes his dictionary is good. The irony is his definitions are just as set and inflexible.*	*sardonic*

*By permission. From *Merriam-Webster's Collegiate® Dictionary, 11th Edition* ©2012 by Merriam-Webster, Incorporated (www.Merriam-Webster.com).

3. Set up student pairs, keeping Speaking and Listening Standard 1 in mind, and assign each pair up to 3 words of the 16 that are presented on the organizer. Explain that each pair should analyze their assigned words, record the analyses on their individual copy of the organizer, and prepare to present their analyses to the rest of the class. Be sure to tell students how much time they will have for this work.

4. Bring the class back together for the word analysis presentations; one possible way to organize the presentations is by literary term (all examples of verbal irony, for example). As their classmates make their reports, students should fill in the remainder of the cells in their organizers, based on the information presented. Depending on time, some presentations might take place in Class #2; be sure to leave time in the class period for the closing/reflection activity.

Close the Lesson

1. Ask students to return to their vocabulary graphic organizer and update their self-assessed understanding of the listed literary terms. They should reflect in writing on how analyzing the definitions altered their understanding of these terms.

Lesson Activity Sequence—Class #2

Start the Lesson

1. Post and discuss the learning objective for Class Session #2: To practice using figures of speech and word choice to convey meaning and tone by writing definitions and presenting them to the class.
2. Ask a few student volunteers to share what they wrote about the literary terms at the close of the previous class session.

Engage Students in Learning the Content

1. If necessary, resume the presentations on students' analysis of the alternative definitions.
2. Explain to students that they will have a set amount of time, working in the same pairs as before, to write their own alternate "playing with words" definitions of some familiar words. Distribute the **Playing with Words Assignment Guidelines** (see **Figure C,** p. 115). Project a copy, review the directions, and remind students to follow the directions as they work. Circulate through the classroom to ensure that the definitions students are generating demonstrate the various figures and literary devices of speech. Also remind them to identify the part of speech associated with each word, as dictionaries do.
3. At the conclusion of the work period, ask students to present and get feedback on their definitions, adhering to the assignment's written guidelines. As each student presents, facilitate the conversation, monitor student understanding, and collect formative data to inform follow-up instruction.

Close the Lesson

1. Wrap up by reviewing the day's learning objectives: to practice using figures of speech and word choice to convey meaning and tone by writing definitions and presenting them to the class.

2. Assign homework: Tell students to study for a short assessment of the vocabulary words *connotation, denotation, hyperbole, metaphor, pun, sarcasm, sardonic
   tone, simile, tone, verbal irony,* and *wit.*

Additional Resources for This Lesson

The following definitions* of key terms may be helpful during direct instruction:

1. **Connotation**—the suggesting of a meaning by a word apart from the thing it explicitly names or describes; something suggested by a word or thing: implication.
2. **Denotation**—a direct specific meaning as distinct from an implied or associated
   idea.
3. **Hyperbole**—extravagant exaggeration.
4. **Metaphor**—a figure of speech in which a word or phrase literally denoting one
   kind of object or idea is used in place of another to suggest a likeness or analogy
   between them *broadly:* figurative language.
5. **Pun**—the usually humorous use of a word in such a way as to suggest two or
   more of its meanings or the meaning of another word similar in sound.
6. **Sarcasm**—a mode of satirical wit depending for its effect on bitter, caustic, and
   often ironic language that is usually directed against an individual.
7. **Sardonic tone**—disdainfully or skeptically humorous: derisively mocking.
8. **Simile**—a figure of speech comparing two unlike things that is often introduced
   by *like* or *as* (as in *cheeks like roses*)
9. **Tone**—style or manner of expression in speaking or writing.
10. **Verbal irony**—the use of words to express something other than and especially
    the opposite of the literal meaning; a usually humorous or sardonic literary
    style or form characterized by irony.
11. **Wit**—a form of intellectual humor; clever or apt humor.

For additional dictionaries that complement this lesson's resources, see the website "Strange and Unusual References" (http://www.oneletterwords.com/). One
more dictionary students might enjoy is Zoe and Laura Steele's *The Snot-Nosed Kid's
Dictionary: Clean, If Slightly Germy, Jokes* (Kindle version available from amazon.com).

---

*Definitions by permission. From *Merriam-Webster's Collegiate® Dictionary, 11th Edition* ©2012 by Merriam-
Webster, Incorporated (www.Merriam-Webster.com).

Figure A	**Advance Organizer for Vocabulary Assessment and Development**
Literary Terminology: What Do You Know About These Words?

Rate each of the words below as follows:

1 = I've never heard this word before.
2 = I've heard this word, but I don't know what it means.
3 = I understand the meaning of this word.
4 = I understand this word and can use it in a sentence.

connotation	1	2	3	4	**sardonic tone**	1	2	3	4
denotation	1	2	3	4	**simile**	1	2	3	4
hyperbole	1	2	3	4	**tone**	1	2	3	4
metaphor	1	2	3	4	**verbal irony**	1	2	3	4
pun	1	2	3	4	**wit**	1	2	3	4
sarcasm	1	2	3	4					

For any terms above that you ranked a 3 or 4, please write a definition in your own words.

1. connotation

2. denotation

3. hyperbole

4. metaphor

5. pun

6. sarcasm

7. sardonic tone

8. simile

9. tone

10. verbal irony

11. wit

Figure B	**Graphic Organizer for Definition Analysis**				
Definition from Merriam-Webster's Online Dictionary	Alternative Definitions from *The Devil's Dictionary* and *The Wit's Dictionary*	Which figure(s) of speech does the alternative definition use?	What point is the author making, and how does he employ the identified figure of speech?	What is the author's tone?
1. ACADEMY, *n.* a school usually above the elementary level; *especially:* a private high school. A high school or college in which special subjects or skills are taught.	**ACADEMY,** *n.* [from ACADEME] a modern school where football is taught. (Bierce)			
2. BAGPIPES, *n.* a wind instrument consisting of a reed melody pipe and from one to five drones with air supplied continuously either by a bag with valve-stopped mouth tube or by bellows—often used in plural	**BAGPIPES,** *n.* an octopus with a kilt. (Bowles)			
3. CABBAGE, *n.* any of several brassicas (*Brassica oleracea*) of European origin; *especially:* a leafy garden plant (*Brassica oleracea capitata*) with a short stem and a dense globular head of usually green leaves that is used as a vegetable.	**CABBAGE,** *n.* a familiar kitchen-garden vegetable about as large and wise as a man's head. (Bierce)			

Sources: Column 1: By permission. *Merriam-Webster's Collegiate® Dictionary, 11th Edition* ©2012 by Merriam-Webster, Incorporated (www.Merriam-Webster.com). Column 2, rows 1, 2, 5, 7–11, 13–15 from *The Devil's Dictionary* by Ambrose Bierce, 1911. Retrieved from www.thedevilsdictionary.com. Column 2, rows, 2, 4, 6, 12, 16 from *The Wit's Dictionary* by Colin Bowles, 1986, London, UK: Angus & Robertson. © 1986 by Angus & Robertson. Used with permission.

(continued)

Figure B	Graphic Organizer for Definition Analysis *(continued)*				
Definition from Merriam-Webster's Online Dictionary	Alternative Definitions from *The Devil's Dictionary* and *The Wit's Dictionary*	Which figure(s) of speech does the alternative definition use?	What point is the author making, and how does he employ the identified figure of speech?	What is the author's tone?
4. **COINCIDE,** *v.* to occupy the same place in space or time.	**COINCIDE,** *v.* what you do when it starts to rain. (Bowles)			
5. **COWARD,** *n.* one who shows disgraceful fear or timidity.	**COWARD,** *n.* one who in a perilous emergency thinks with his legs. (Bierce)			
6. **CYNIC,** *n.* a faultfinding captious critic; *especially:* one who believes that human conduct is motivated wholly by self-interest.	**CYNIC,** *n.* a man who found out when he was 10 that there was no Santa Claus and he's still disappointed. (Bowles)			
7. **CYNIC,** n. a faultfinding captious critic; *especially:* one who believes that human conduct is motivated wholly by self-interest.	**CYNIC,** *n.* a blackguard whose faulty vision sees things as they are, not as they ought to be. (Bierce)			
8. **DENTIST,** n. one who is skilled in and licensed to practice the prevention, diagnosis, and treatment of diseases, injuries, and malformations of the teeth, jaws, and mouth and who makes and inserts false teeth.	**DENTIST,** *n.* a prestidigitator who, putting metal into your mouth, pulls coins out of your pocket. (Bierce)			

Figure B **Graphic Organizer for Definition Analysis** *(continued)*					
Definition from Merriam-Webster's Online Dictionary	Alternative Definitions from *The Devil's Dictionary* and *The Wit's Dictionary*	Which figure(s) of speech does the alternative definition use?	What point is the author making, and how does he employ the identified figure of speech?	What is the author's tone?
9. **HAPPINESS,** *n.* a state of well-being and contentment: joy; a pleasurable or satisfying experience.	**HAPPINESS,** *n.* an agreeable sensation arising from contemplating the misery of another. (Bierce)			
10. **HISTORIAN,** *n.* a student or writer of history.	**HISTORIAN,** *n.* a broad-gauge gossip. (Bierce)			
11. **IDIOT,** *n.* a foolish or stupid person.	**IDIOT,** *n.* a member of a large and powerful tribe whose influence in human affairs has always been dominant and controlling. The Idiot's activity is not confined to any special field of thought or action, but "pervades and regulates the whole." He has the last word in everything; his decision is unappealable. He sets the fashions and opinion of taste, dictates the limitations of speech and circumscribes conduct with a dead-line. (Bierce)			
12. **IMPALED,** *v.* to pierce with or as if with something pointed; *especially:* to torture or kill by fixing on a sharp stake	**IMPALED,** *adj.* getting the wrong end of the stick. (Bowles)			

(continued)

Figure B	**Graphic Organizer for Definition Analysis** *(continued)*				
Definition from Merriam-Webster's Online Dictionary	Alternative Definitions from *The Devil's Dictionary* and *The Wit's Dictionary*	Which figure(s) of speech does the alternative definition use?	What point is the author making, and how does he employ the identified figure of speech?	What is the author's tone?
13. **LAUGHTER,** *n.* a sound of or as if of laughing. Synonym: belly laugh.	**LAUGHTER,** *n.* an interior convulsion, producing a distortion of the features and accompanied by inarticulate noises. It is infectious and, though intermittent, incurable. (Bierce)			
14. **OYSTER,** *n.* any of various marine bivalve mollusks (family *Ostreidae*) that have a rough irregular shell closed by a single adductor muscle and include commercially important shellfish.	**OYSTER,** *n.* a slimy, gobby shellfish which civilization gives men the hardihood to eat without removing its entrails! (Bierce)			
15. **TELEPHONE,** *n.* an instrument for reproducing sounds at a distance; *specifically:* one in which sound is converted into electrical impulses for transmission (as by wire or radio waves).	**TELEPHONE,** *n.* an invention of the devil which abrogates some of the advantages of making a disagreeable person keep his distance. (Bierce)			
16. **UPPER CRUST,** *n.* the highest social class or group; *especially:* the highest circle of the upper class	**UPPER CRUST,** *n.* a lot of crumbs held together by dough. (Bowles, paraphrasing author Jean Webster)			

Figure C | **Playing with Words Assignment Guidelines**

Independent Application Activity

1. Think about the different figures of speech that we have defined, examined, and discussed during this lesson, and choose two that you are interested in illustrating:

❑ hyperbole   ❑ sarcasm   ❑ verbal irony

❑ metaphor   ❑ sardonic tone   ❑ wit

❑ pun   ❑ simile

2. Choose at least two of the following words to define in a manner that illustrates your chosen figure of speech. (For example, you might create a definition for *smartphone,* used as a verb, that illustrates *hyperbole.*)

❑ car   ❑ library   ❑ smartphone

❑ Internet   ❑ middle school   ❑ teenager

❑ job   ❑ school picture   ❑ test/exam

3. Create an alternative definition for each of the words you've selected, illustrating a different figure of speech in each definition. Make sure you

❑ know the meaning you want to communicate in each definition.

❑ choose words and adjust your tone to communicate that point.

❑ include the word's part of speech within each definition (noun, verb, adjective, etc.).

❑ indicate the figure of speech each definition is demonstrating.

Whole-Class Discussion

4. Present each of your words, its part of speech, its definition, and the figure of speech your definition is demonstrating.

5. Get feedback from the rest of the class:

❑ What point do they think you are trying to make with your definition? Why do they think that?

❑ Do they agree that each definition illustrates the figure of speech you intended it illustrate? Why or why not?

❑ How would they describe your tone? What words do they think help to create that tone?

References

Coleman, D., & Pimentel, S. (2012). *Revised publishers' criteria for the Common Core State Standards in English language arts and literacy, grades 3–12*. Retrieved from http://www.corestandards.org/assets/Publishers_Criteria_for_3-12.pdf

Common Core State Standards Initiative. (2010a). *Application of Common Core State Standards for English language learners*. Washington, DC: CCSSO & National Governors Association. Retrieved from http://www.corestandards.org/assets/application-for-english-learners.pdf

Common Core State Standards Initiative. (2010b). *Application to students with disabilities*. Washington, DC: CCSSO & National Governors Association. Retrieved from http://www.corestandards.org/assets/application-to-students-with-disabilities.pdf

Common Core State Standards Initiative. (2010c). *Common Core State Standards for English language arts & literacy in history/social studies, science, and technical subjects*. Washington, DC: CCSSO & National Governors Association. Retrieved from http://www.corestandards.org/assets/CCSSI_ELA%20Standards.pdf

Common Core State Standards Initiative. (2010d). *Common Core State Standards for English language arts & literacy in history/social studies, science, and technical subjects. Appendix A: Research supporting key elements of the standards, glossary of key terms*. Washington, DC: CCSSO & National Governors Association. Retrieved from http://www.corestandards.org/assets/Appendix_A.pdf

Common Core State Standards Initiative. (2010e). *Common Core State Standards for English language arts & literacy in history/social studies, science, and technical subjects. Appendix B: Text exemplars and sample performance tasks*. Washington, DC: CCSSO & National Governors Association. Retrieved from http://www.corestandards.org/assets/Appendix_B.pdf

Common Core State Standards Initiative. (2010f). *Common Core State Standards for English language arts & literacy in history/social studies, science, and technical subjects. Appendix C: Samples of student writing.* Washington, DC: CCSSO & National Governors Association. Retrieved from http://www.corestandards.org/assets/Appendix_C.pdf

Dean, C. B., Hubbell, E. R., Pitler, H., & Stone, B. (2012). *Classroom instruction that works: Research-based strategies for increasing student achievement* (2nd ed.). Alexandria, VA: ASCD.

Hess, K., (2011, December). *Learning progressions frameworks designed for use with the Common Core State Standards in English language arts & literacy K–12.* Retrieved from http://www.nciea.org/publication_PDFs/ELA_LPF_12%202011_final.pdf

Hess, K. (2012, January). *Content specifications with content mapping for the summative assessment of the Core State Standards for English language arts & literacy in history/social studies, science, and technical subject* [draft]. Retrieved from http://www.smarterbalanced.org/smarter-balanced-assessments/

Hess, K., & Hervey, S. (2011). *Tools for examining text complexity.* Retrieved from http://www.nciea.org/publication_PDFs/Updated%20toolkit-text%20complexity_KH12.pdf

Kansas State Department of Education. (2011). *Text complexity resources.* Retrieved from http://www.ksde.org/Default.aspx?tabid=4778#TextRes

Kendall, J. S. (2011). *Understanding Common Core State Standards.* Alexandria, VA: ASCD.

Measured Progress & ETS Collaborative. (2012, April). Smarter Balanced Assessment Consortium: English language arts item and task specifications. Retrieved from http://www.smarterbalanced.org/smarter-balanced-assessments/#item

National Assessment Governing Board, U.S. Department of Education. (2011). *Writing framework for the 2011 National Assessment of Educational Progress.* Retrieved from http://www.eric.ed.gov/PDFS/ED512552.pdf

Nelson, J., Perfetti, C., Liben, D., & Liben, M. (2012). *Measures of text difficulty: Testing their predictive value for grade levels and student performance.* Retrieved from http://www.ccsso.org/Documents/2012/Measures%20ofText%20Difficulty_final.2012.pdf

Partnership for Assessment of Readiness for College and Careers. (2010). *Application for the* Race to the Top *comprehension assessment systems competition.* Retrieved from http://www.parcconline.org/sites/parcc/files/PARCC%20Application%20-%20FINAL.pdf

Partnership for Assessment of Readiness for College and Careers. (2011, November). *PARCC model content frameworks: English language arts/literacy, grades 3–11.* Retrieved from http://www.parcconline.org/sites/parcc/files/PARCC%20MCF%20for%20ELA%20Literacy_Fall%202011%20Release%20%28rev%29.pdf

About the Authors

Susan Ryan is a senior consultant at Mid-continent Research for Education and Learning (McREL). She has reviewed, revised, and developed language arts standards documents for many districts, state agencies, and education organizations. Ms. Ryan has conducted alignment reviews on assessment items, instructional materials, and curriculum materials. Her work with the Common Core State Standards includes the production of gap analyses, crosswalks, transition documents, alignment reviews, and research support for state departments of education. Ms. Ryan has also facilitated teacher leaders in curriculum development and implementation of the Common Core. She was a consulting state content expert for English language arts during the development of the Common Core and a state consultant to the Partnership for Assessment of Readiness for College and Careers (PARCC) consortium. A former high school language arts teacher, she holds a BA in English from the University of Colorado and a secondary teaching license through Metropolitan State University of Denver.

Dana Frazee is a principal consultant at McREL. She conducts workshops and training on curriculum and system improvement. She works with districts and teachers in North Dakota and Wyoming on the implementation of the Common Core English Language Arts standards. Ms. Frazee has been a middle school and high school teacher, a teacher leader, the principal of a K–8 charter school, and a K–12 educational consultant. She has facilitated numerous regional and national workshops on a variety of subjects, including data-based decision making, writing in the content area, formative assessment, continuous school improvement, and effective instructional strategies. Ms. Frazee coauthored *Teaching Reading in the Content Area,* 3rd edition (2012) and McREL's *Math in Afterschool: An Instructor's Guide to the Afterschool Training Toolkit* (2008). She earned her bachelor's degree from the University of Colorado at Boulder and her master's degree from Adams State College, Colorado.

John Kendall (Series Editor) is Senior Director in Research at McREL in Denver. Having joined McREL in 1988, Mr. Kendall conducts research and development activities related to academic standards. He directs a technical assistance unit that provides standards-related services to schools, districts, states, and national and international organizations. He is the author of *Understanding Common Core State Standards,* the senior author of *Content Knowledge: A Compendium of Standards and Benchmarks for K–12 Education,* and the author or coauthor of numerous reports and guides related to standards-based systems. These works include *High School Standards and Expectations for College and the Workplace, Essential Knowledge: The Debate over What American Students Should Know,* and *Finding the Time to Learn: A Guide.* He holds an MA in Classics and a BA in English Language and Literature from the University of Colorado at Boulder.

About McREL

Mid-continent Research for Education and Learning (McREL) is a nationally recognized nonprofit education research and development organization headquartered in Denver, Colorado, with offices in Honolulu, Hawaii, and Omaha, Nebraska. Since 1966, McREL has helped translate research and professional wisdom about what works in education into practical guidance for educators. Our more than 120 staff members and affiliates include respected researchers, experienced consultants, and published writers who provide educators with research-based guidance, consultation, and professional development for improving student outcomes.